SPANKING TAILS 3

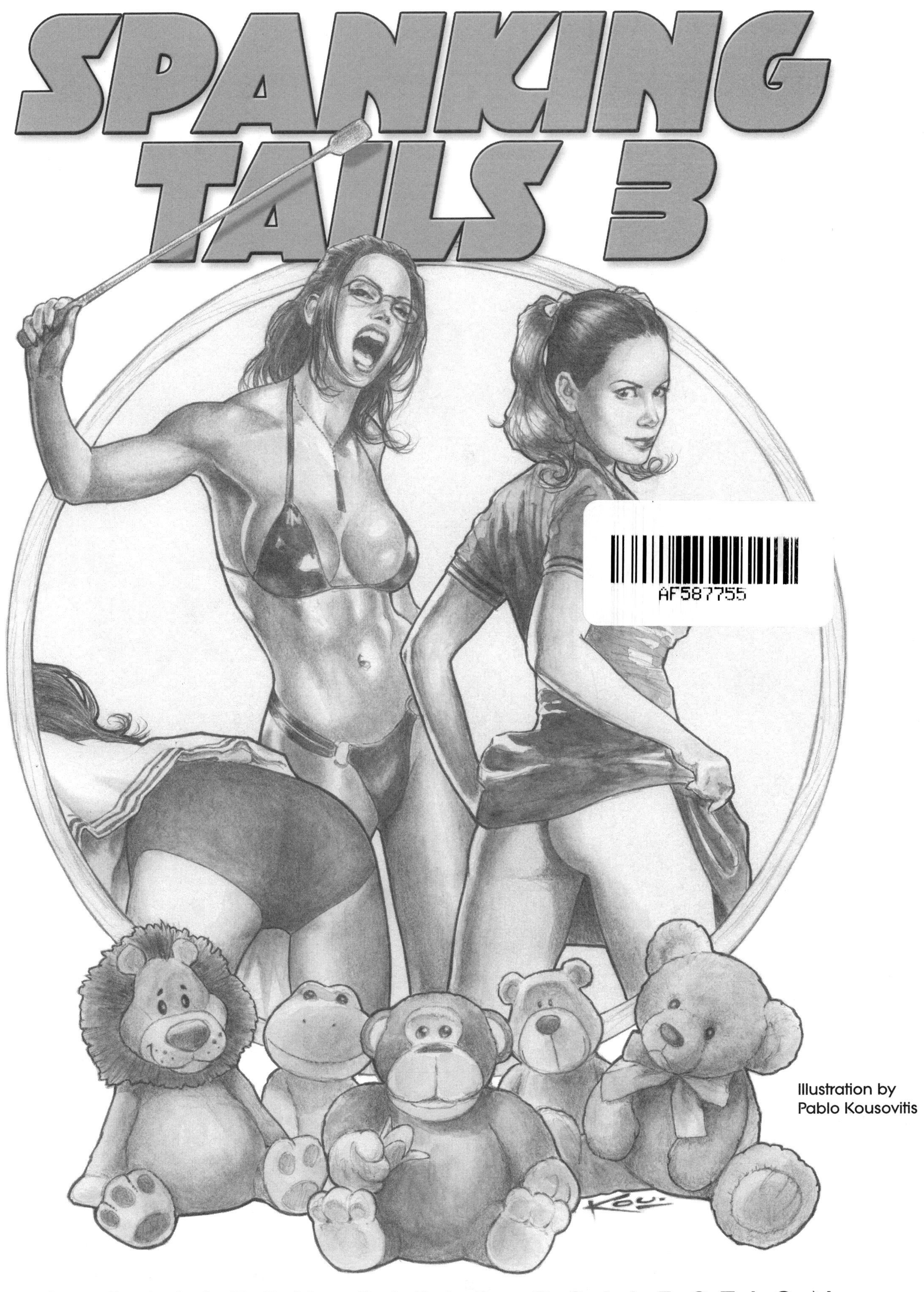

Illustration by
Pablo Kousovitis

A GALLERY GIRLS COLLECTION

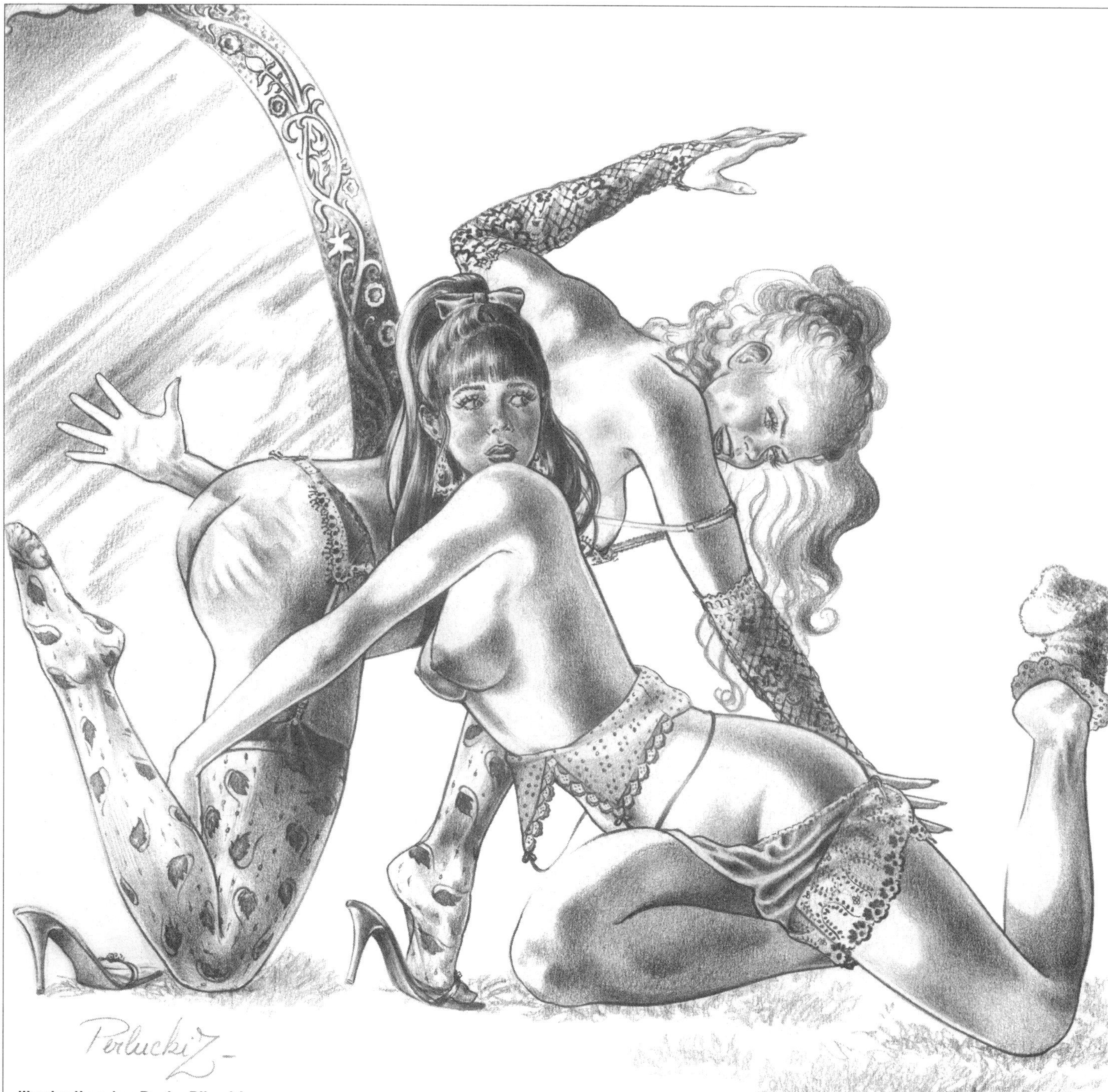

Illustration by Perla Pilucki

SPANKING TAILS

Volume Three

Book design by Grassy Knoll Studios.

Published by
SQP Inc.
PO Box 248 - Columbus, NJ 08022

Sal Quartuccio & Bob Keenan - Publishers

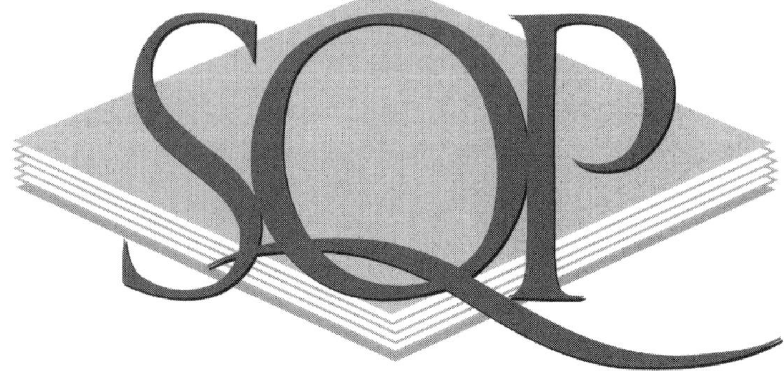

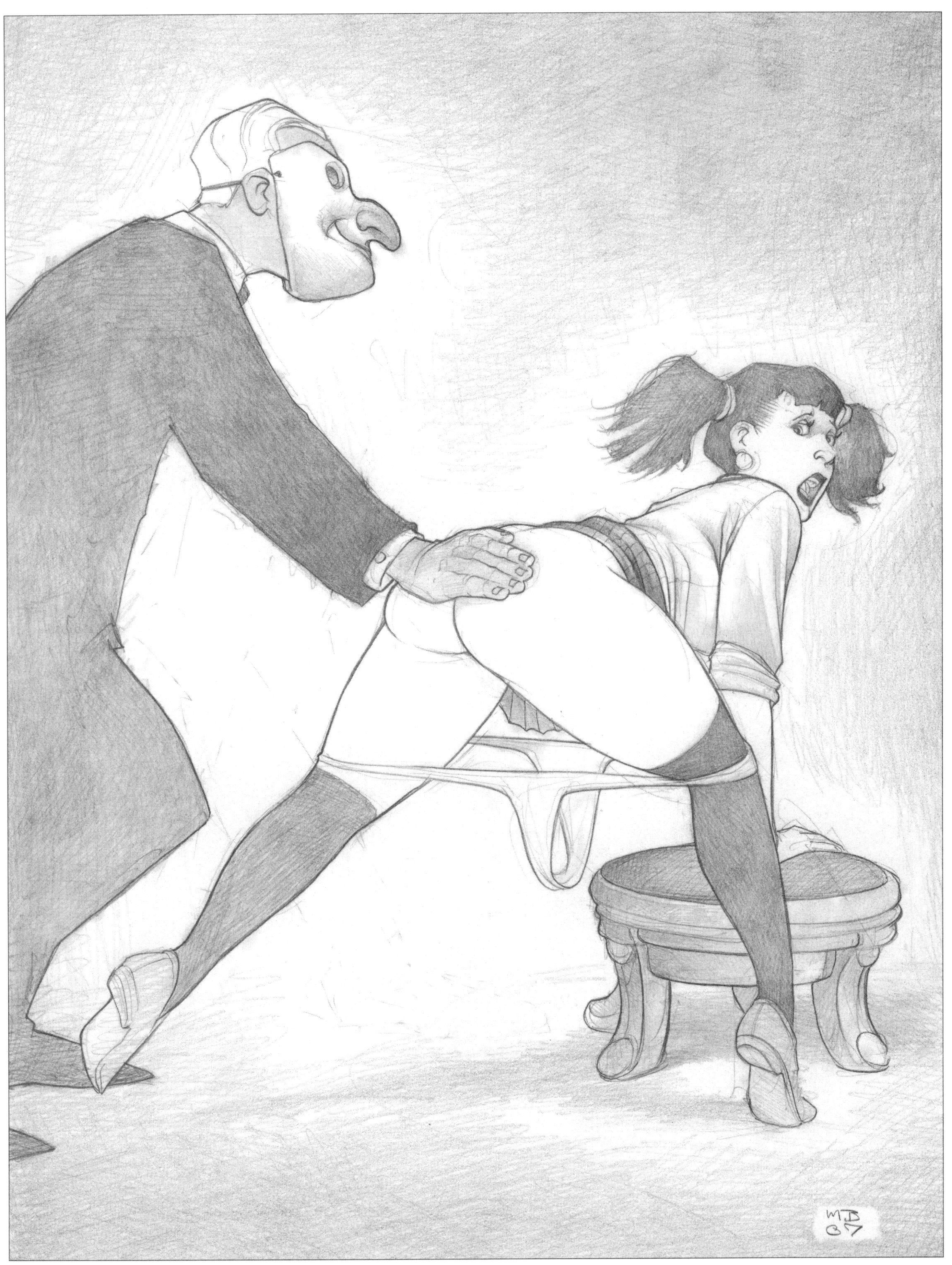

Mitch Byrd

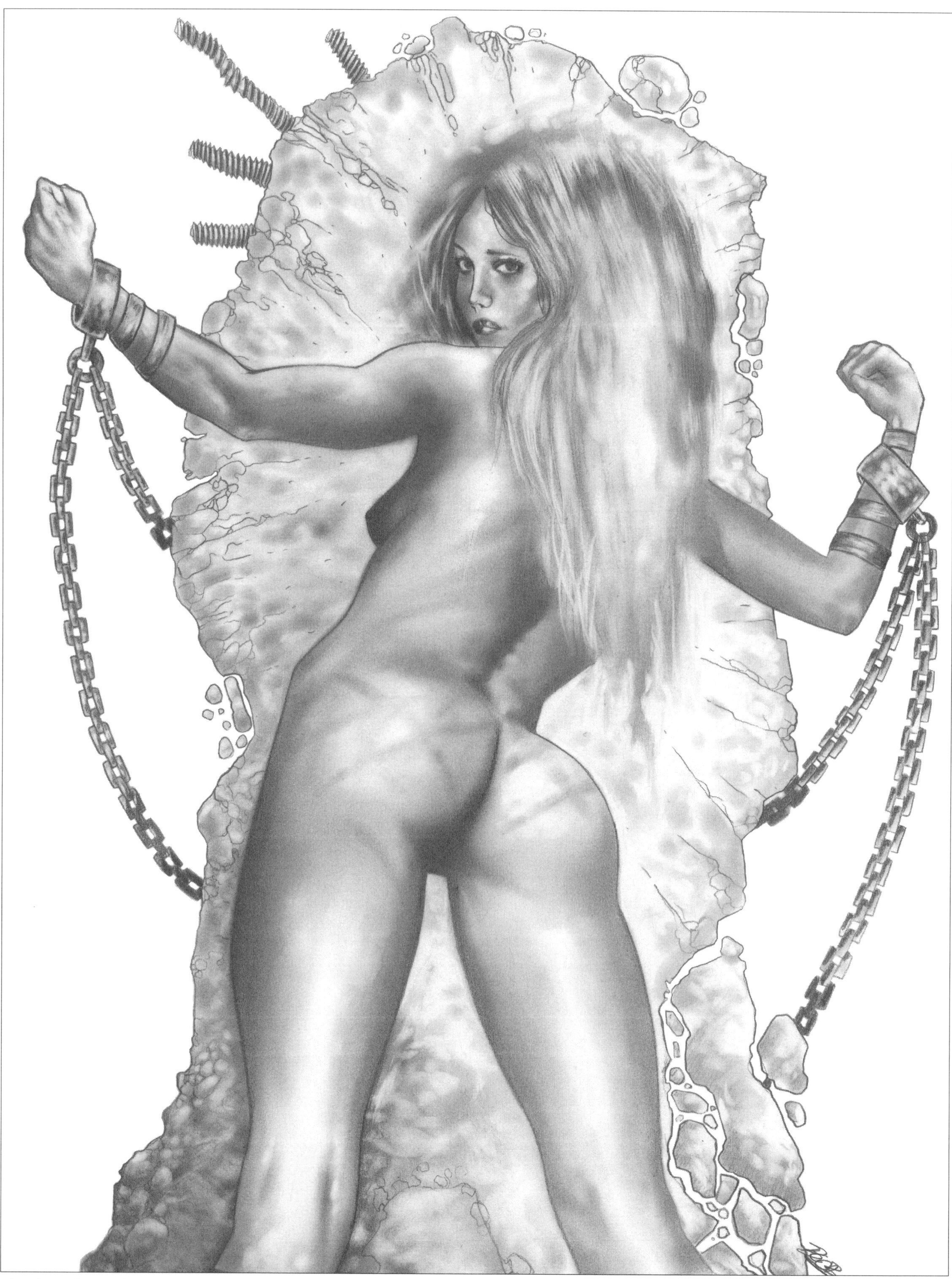

Luis Buci

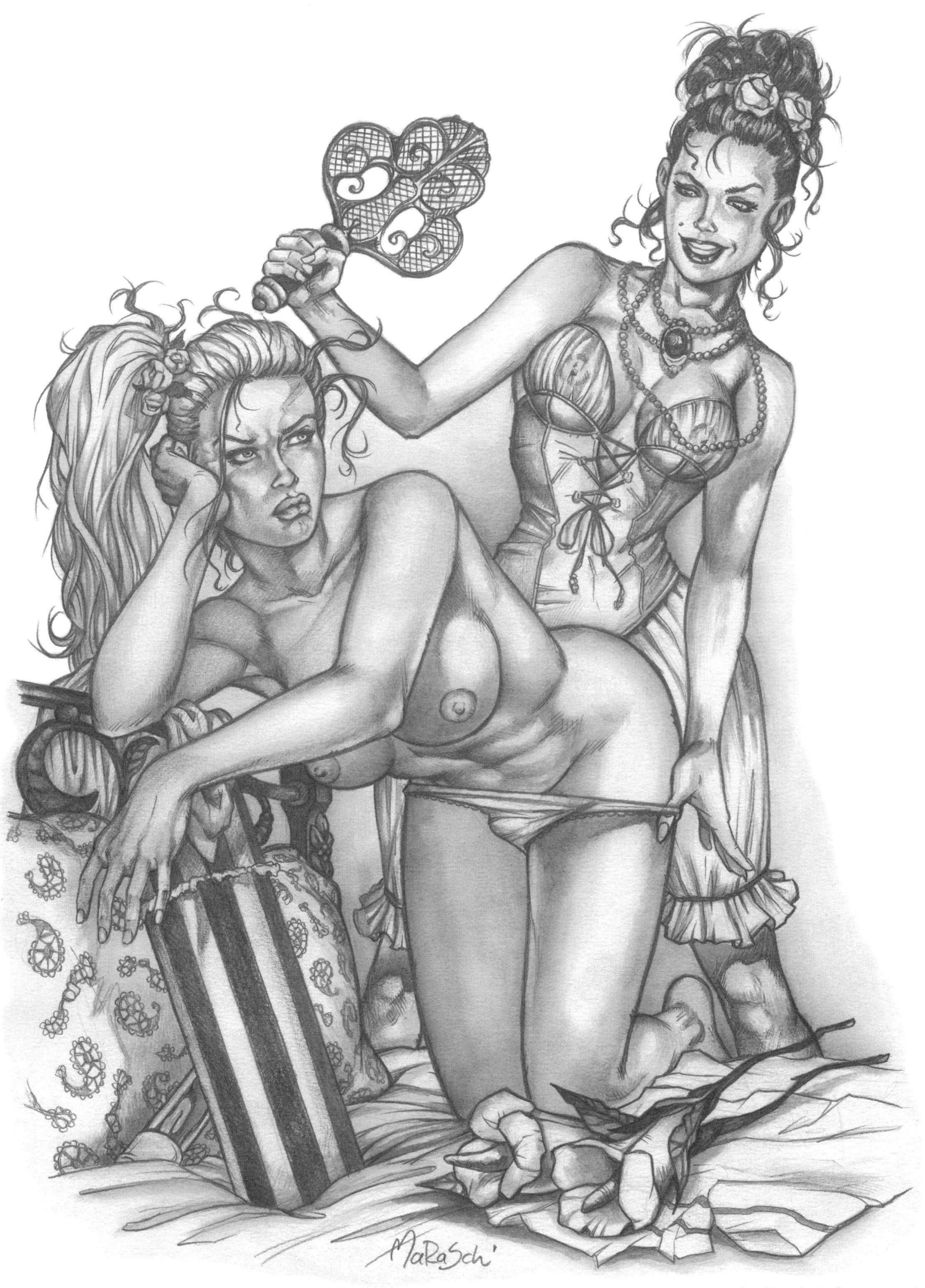

Anibal Maraschi

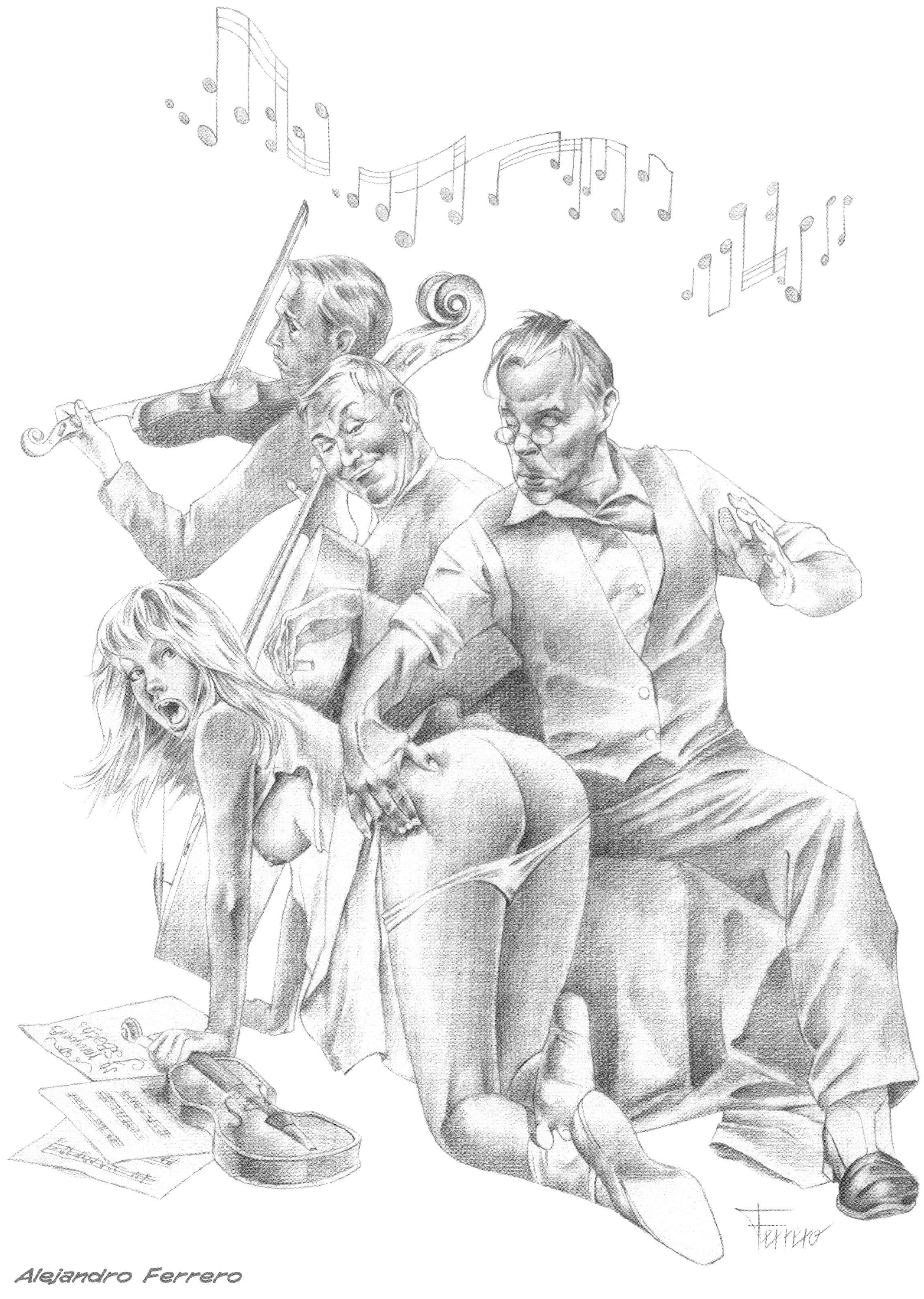

Alejandro Ferrero

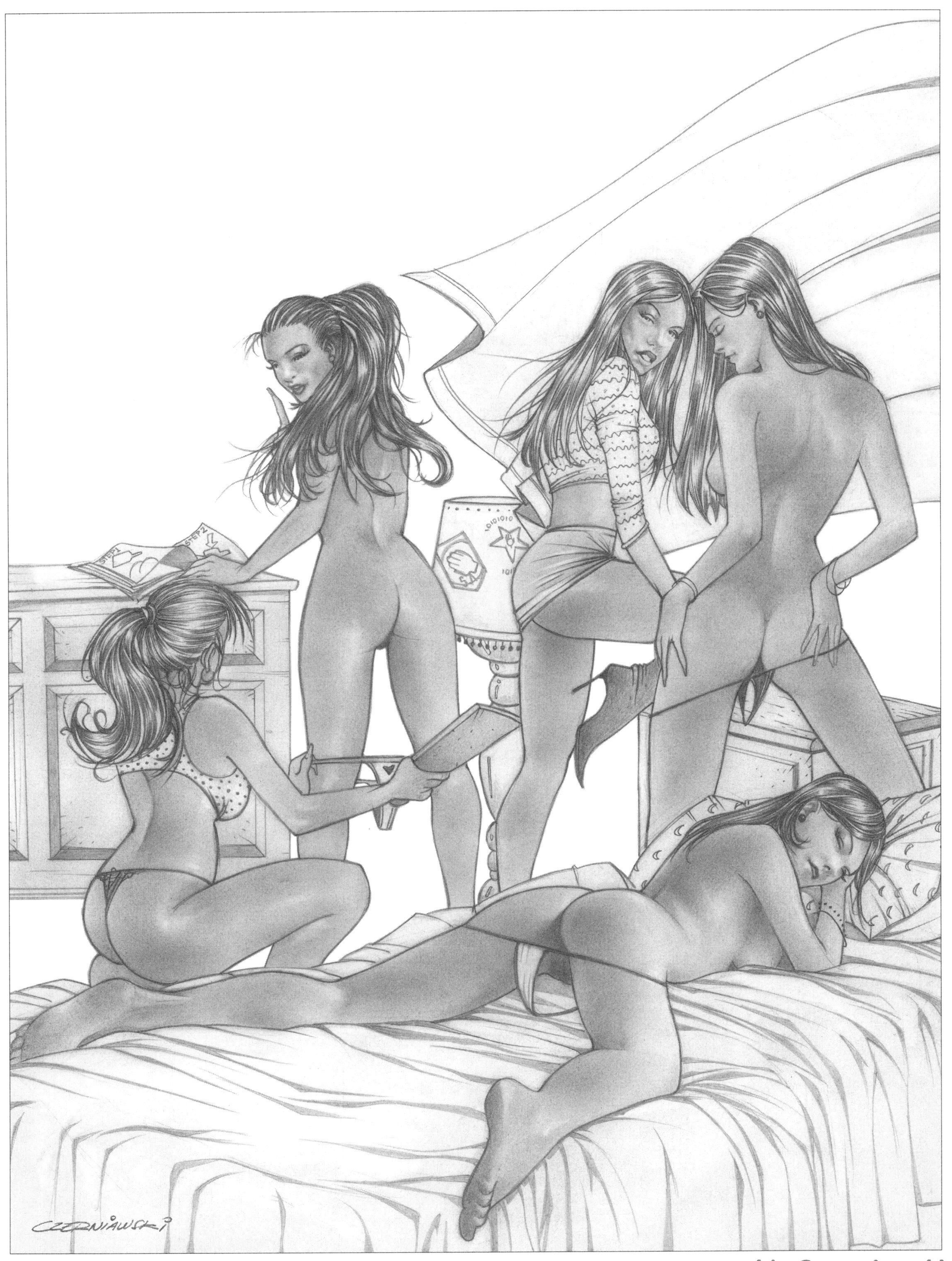

J.L. Czerniawski

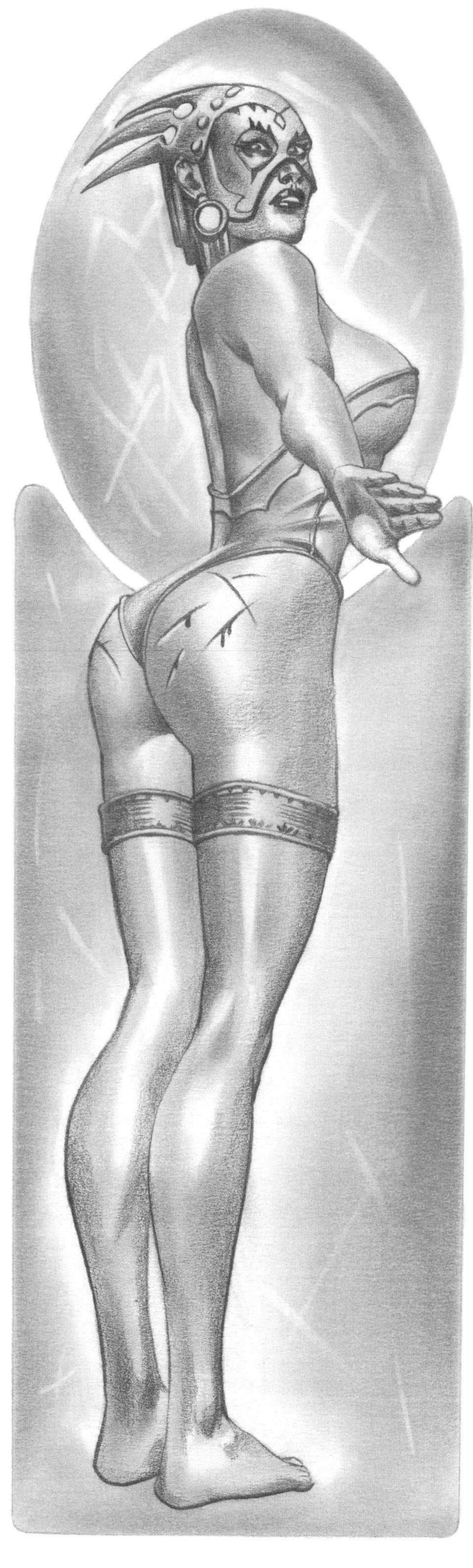

Gonzalo Flores

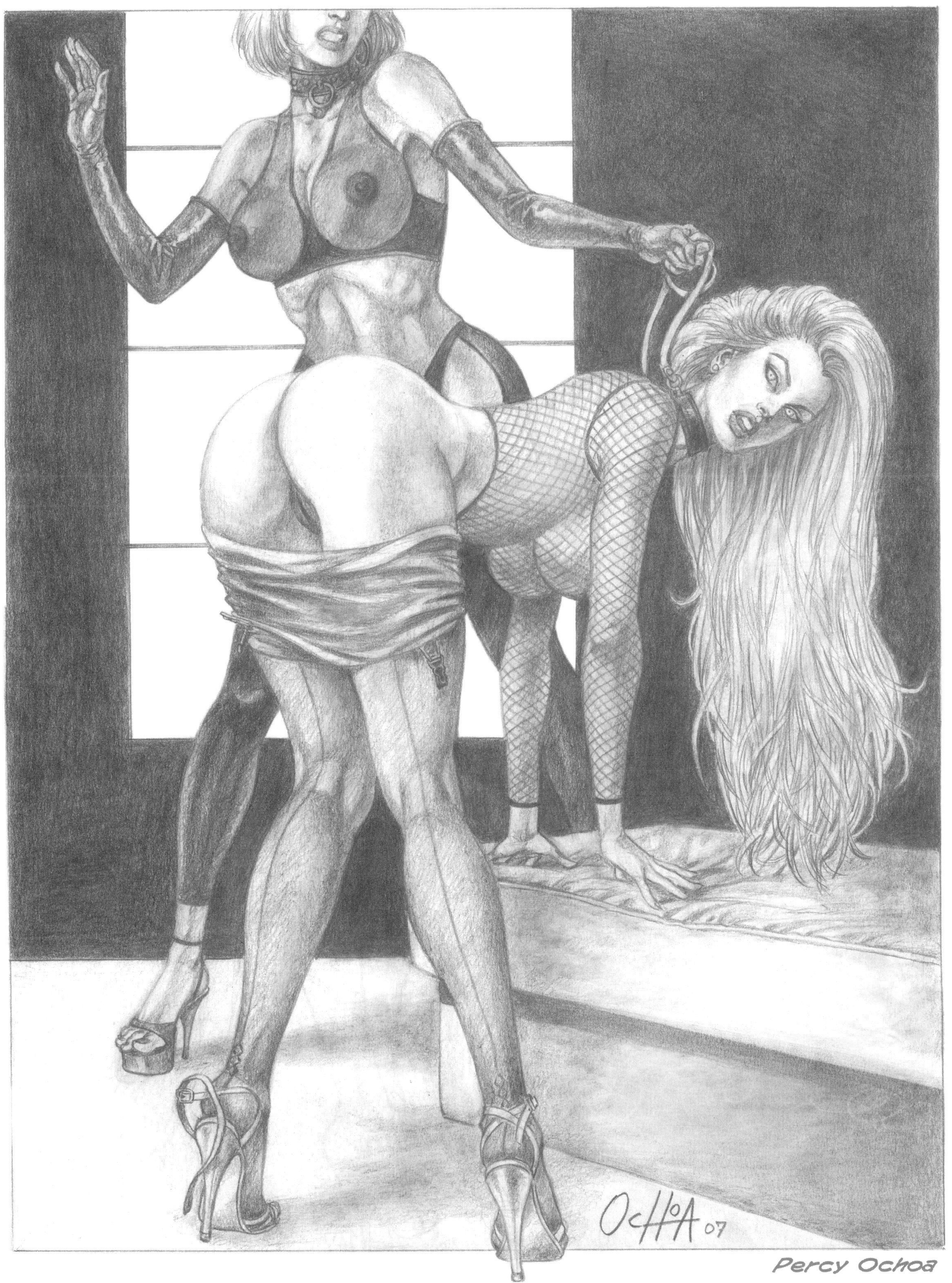

Percy Ochoa

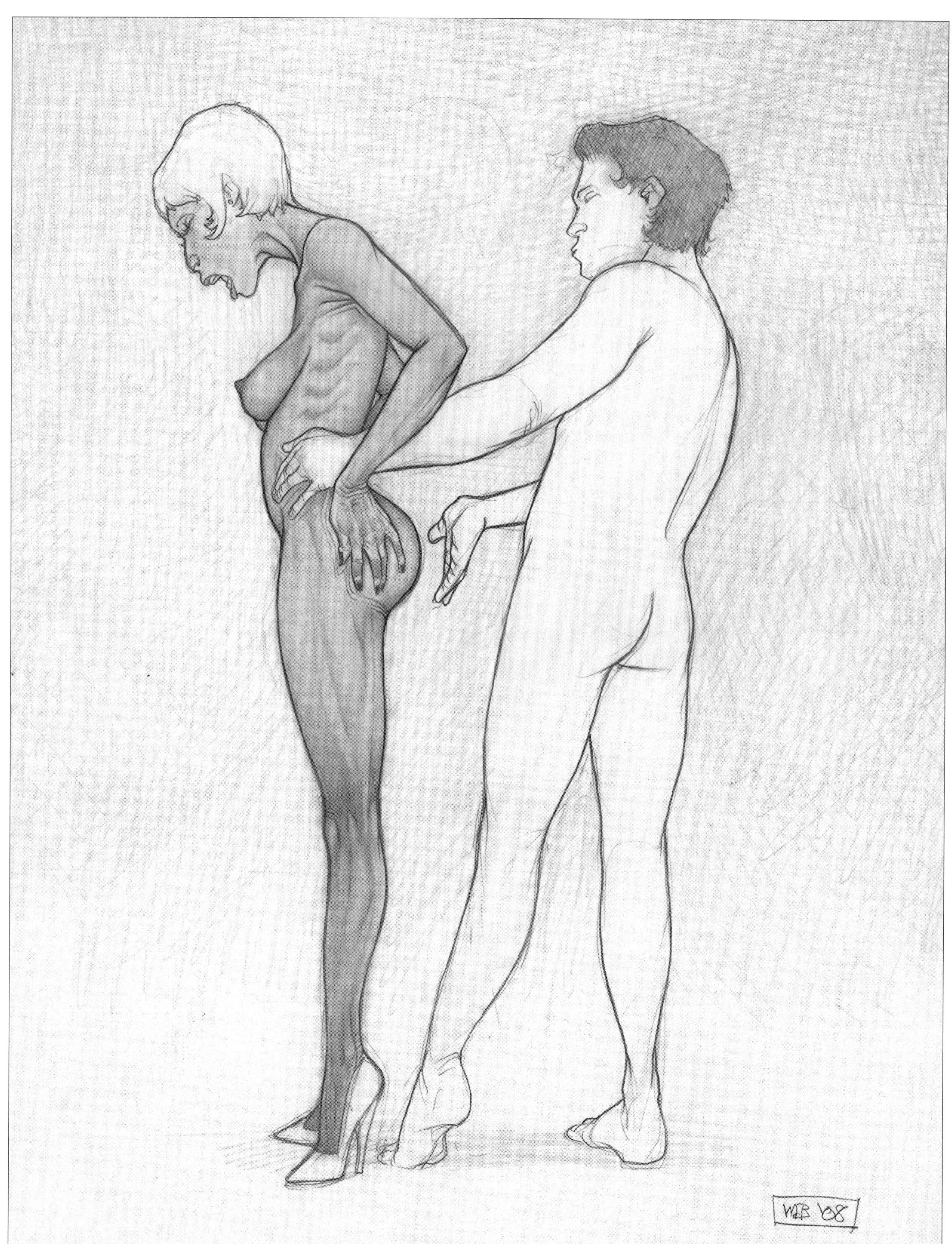

Mitch Byrd

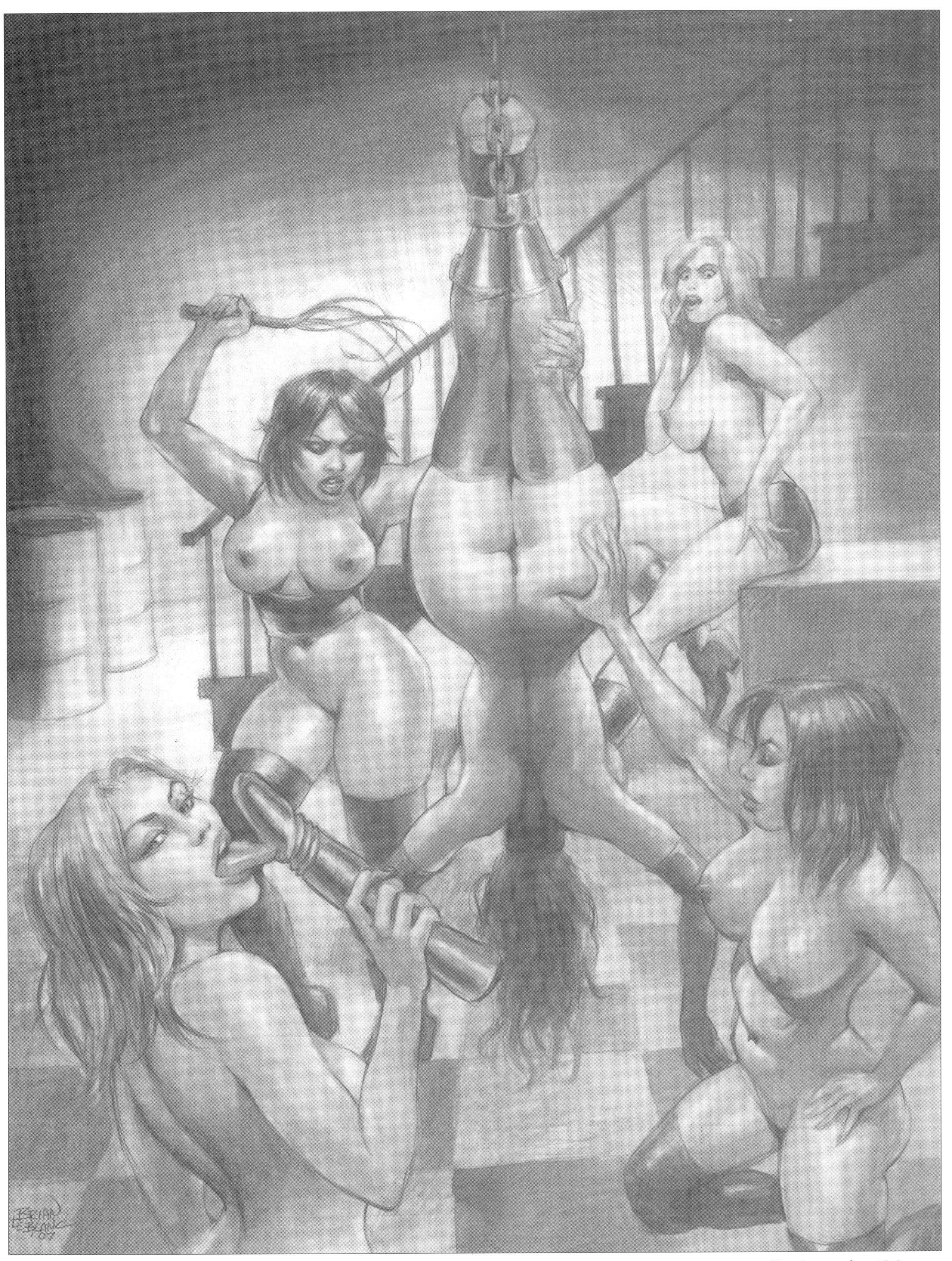

Brian LeBlanc

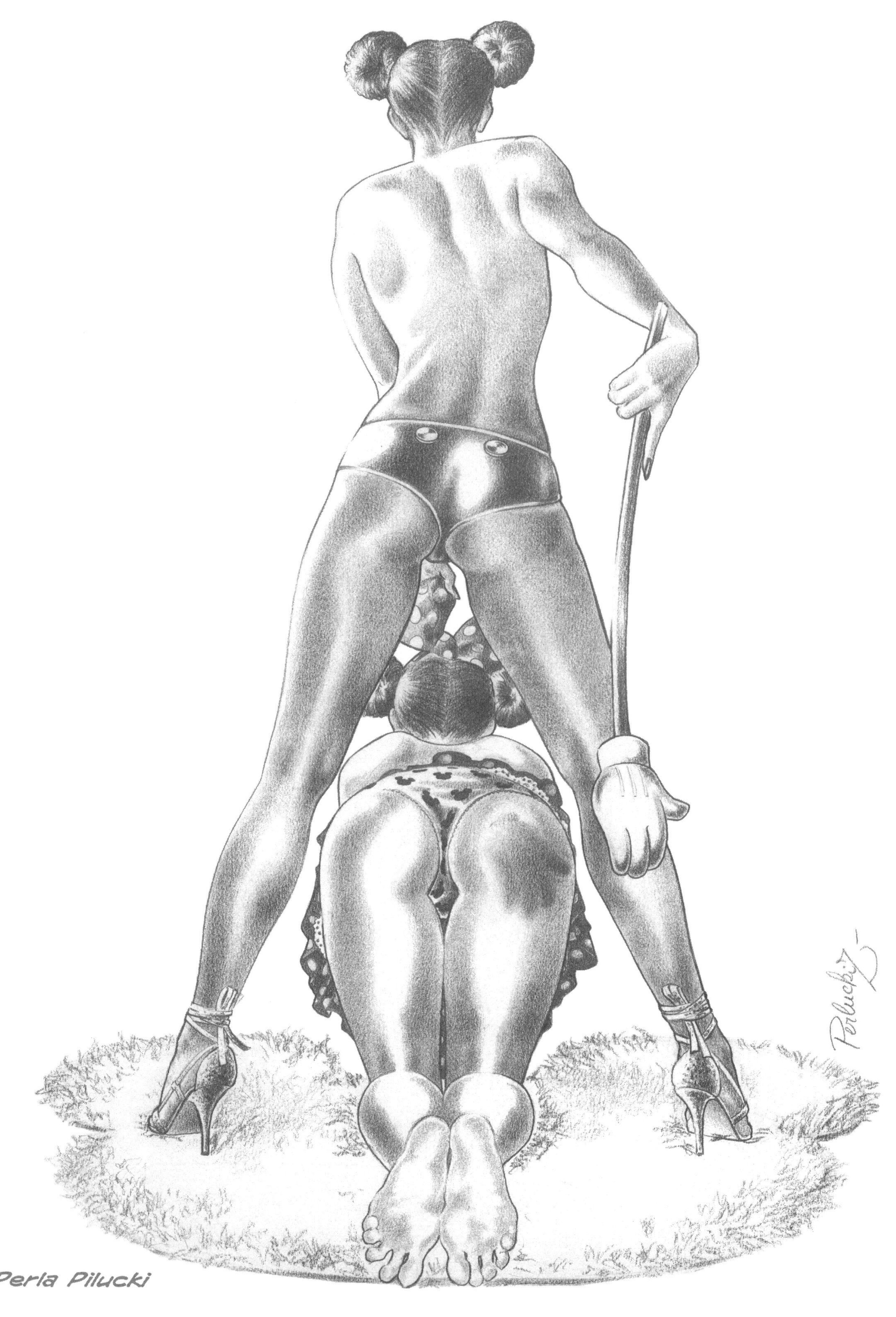

Perla Pilucki

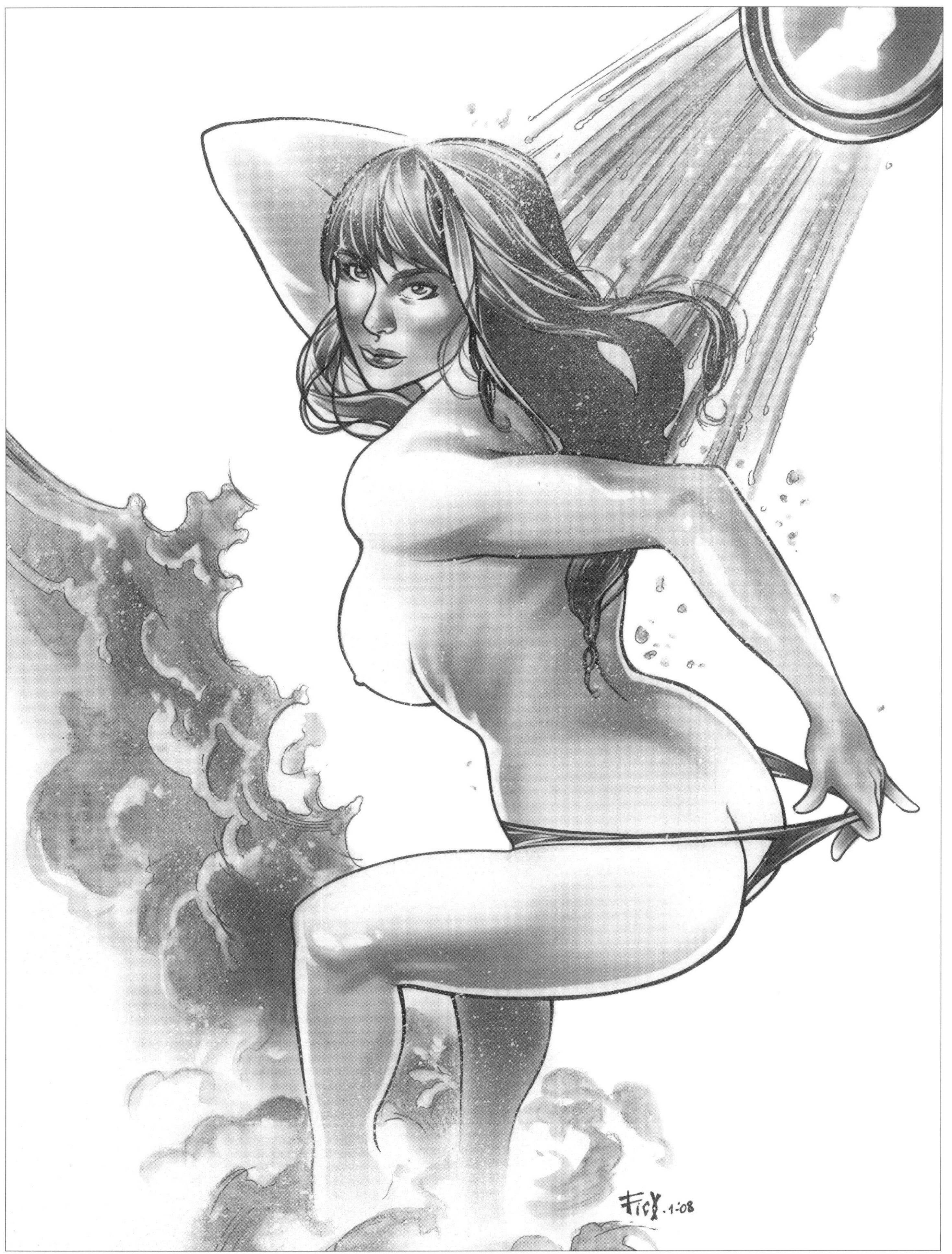

Federico Ossio

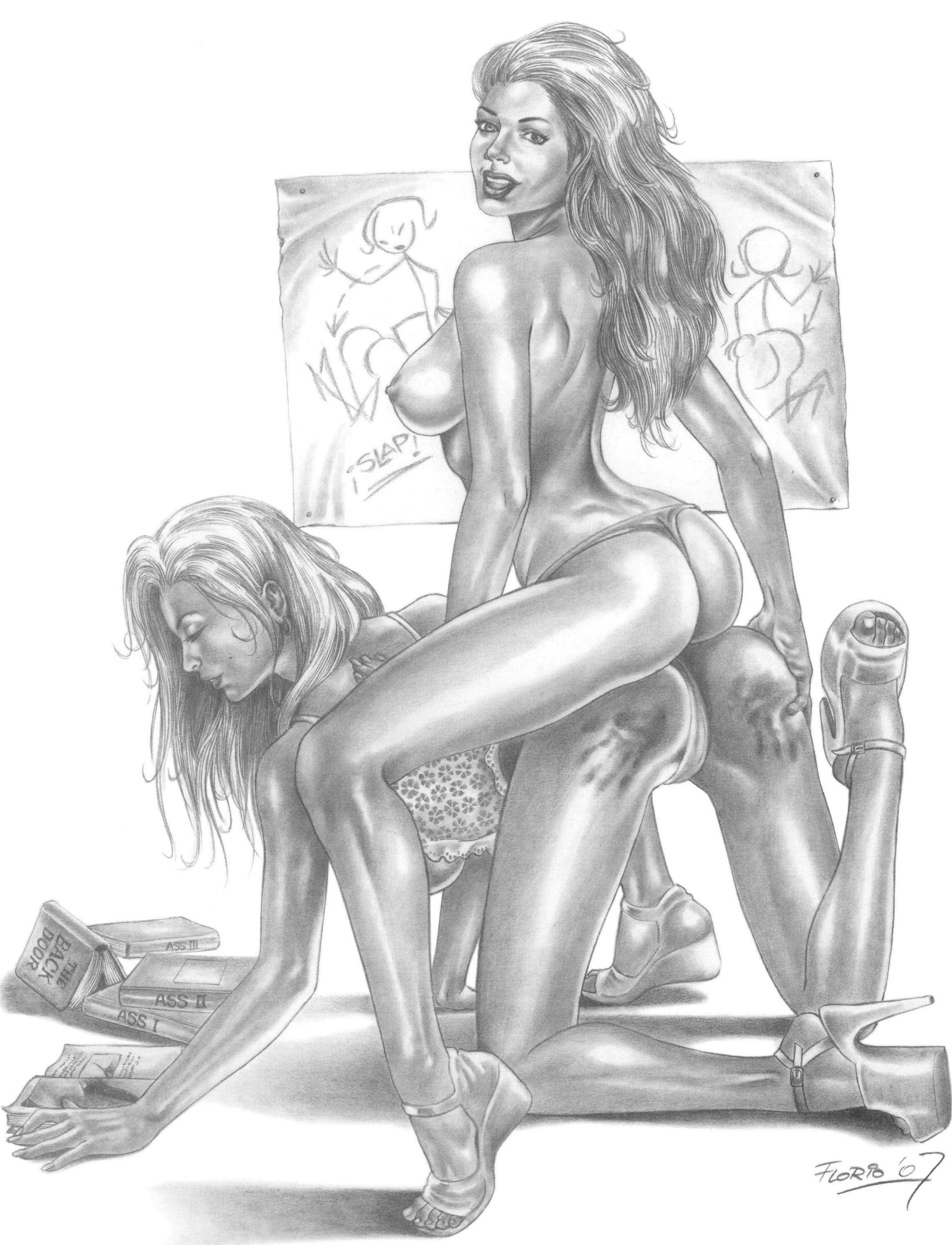

Diego Florio

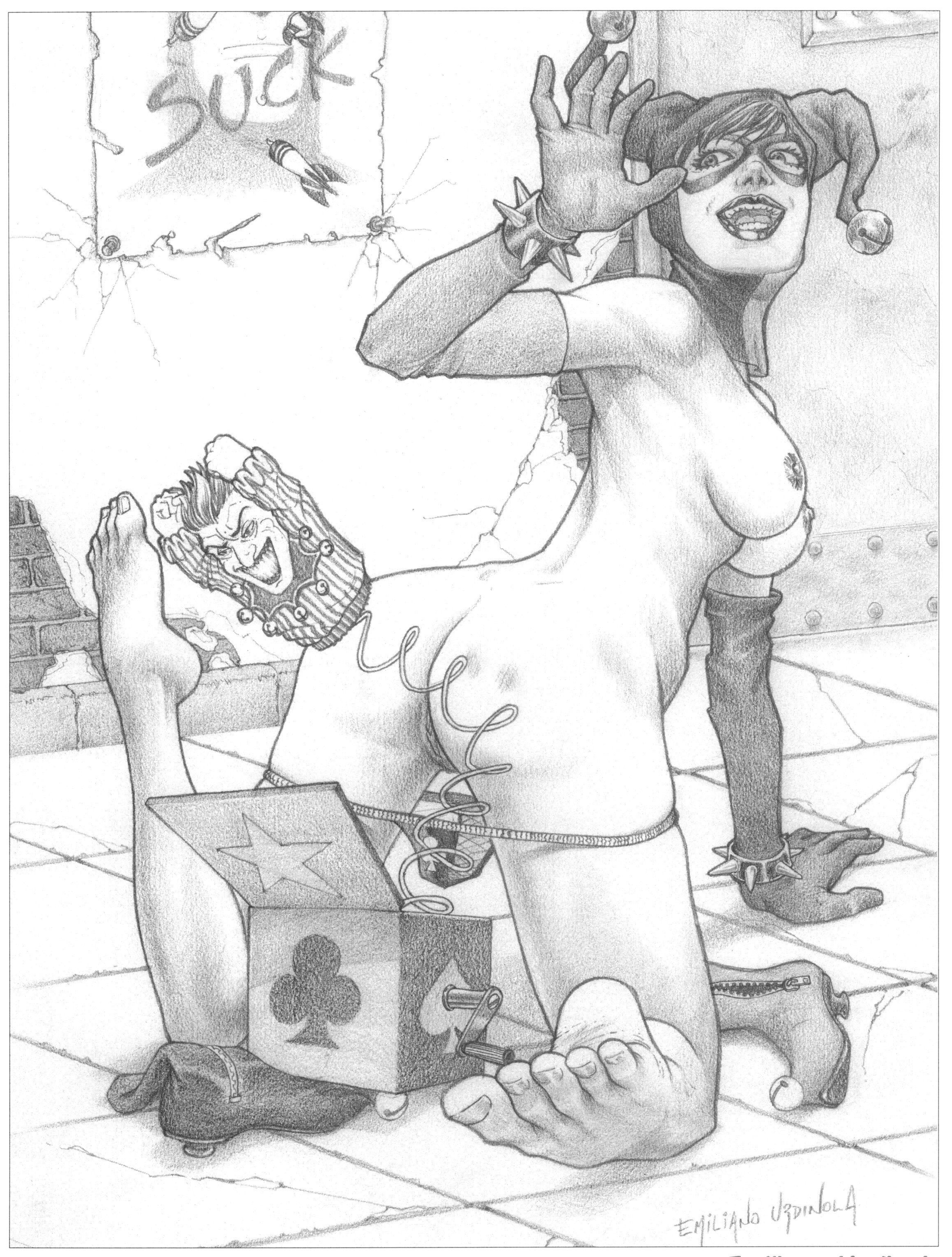

Emiliano Urdinola

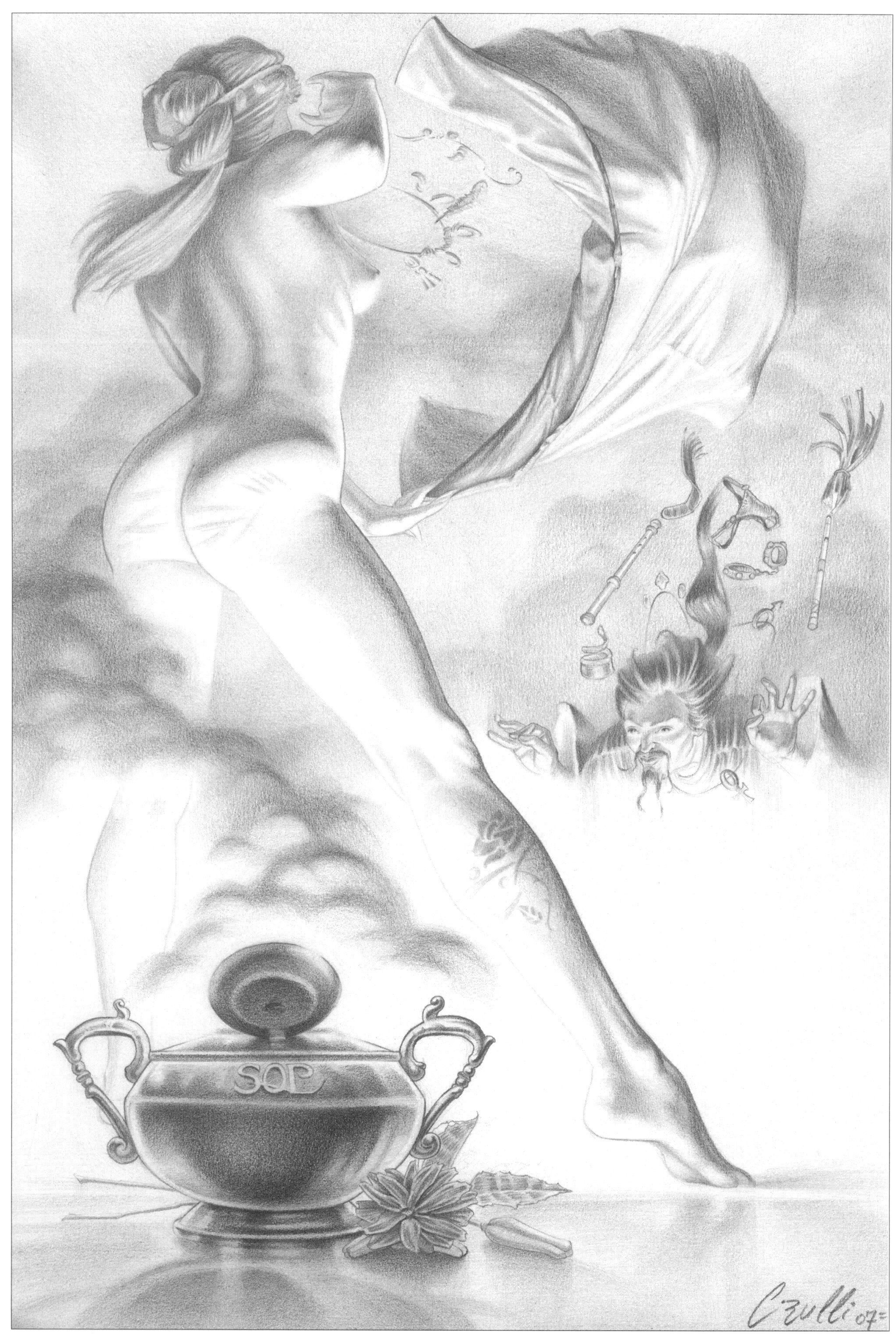

Diego Cirulli

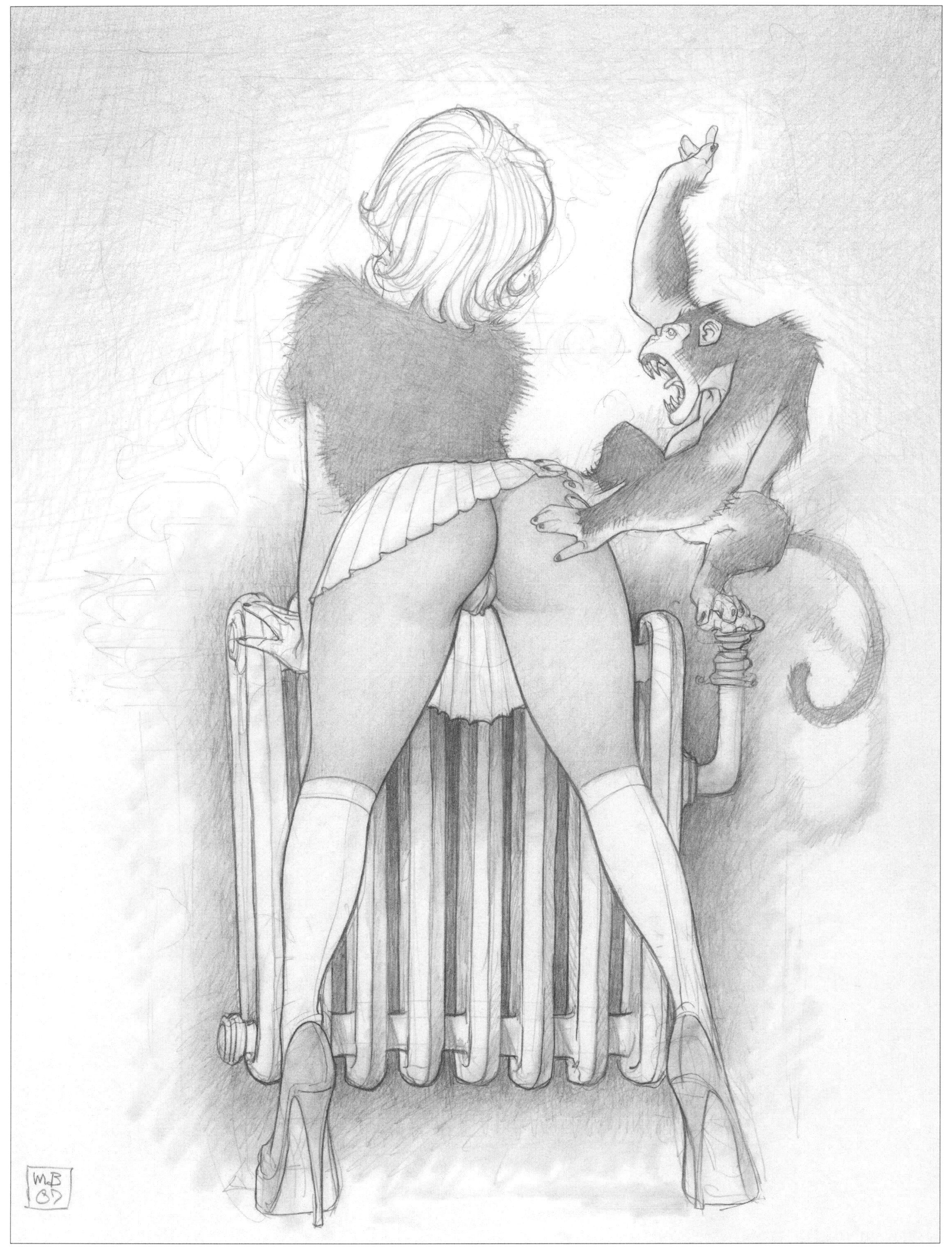

Mitch Byrd

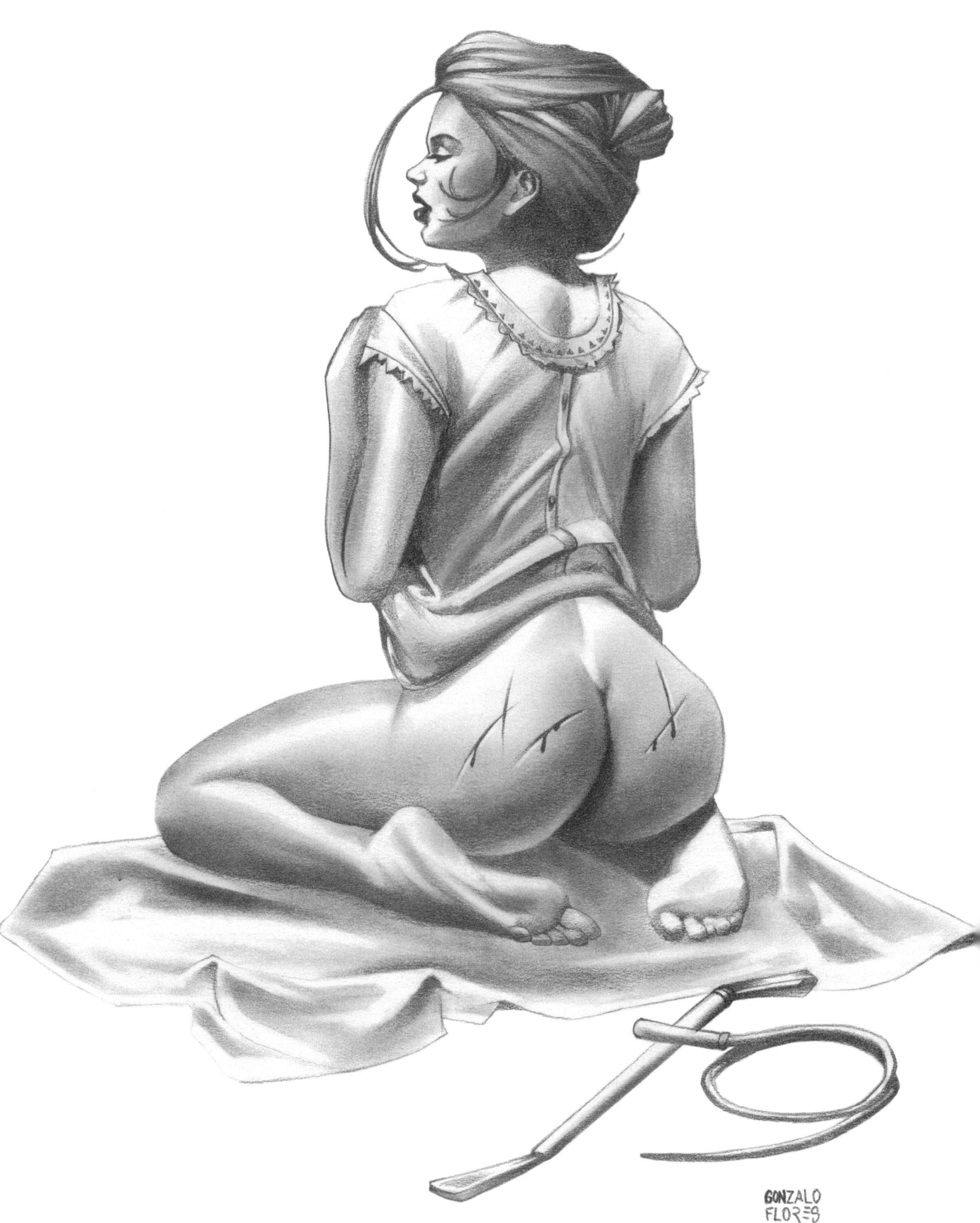

Gonzalo Flores

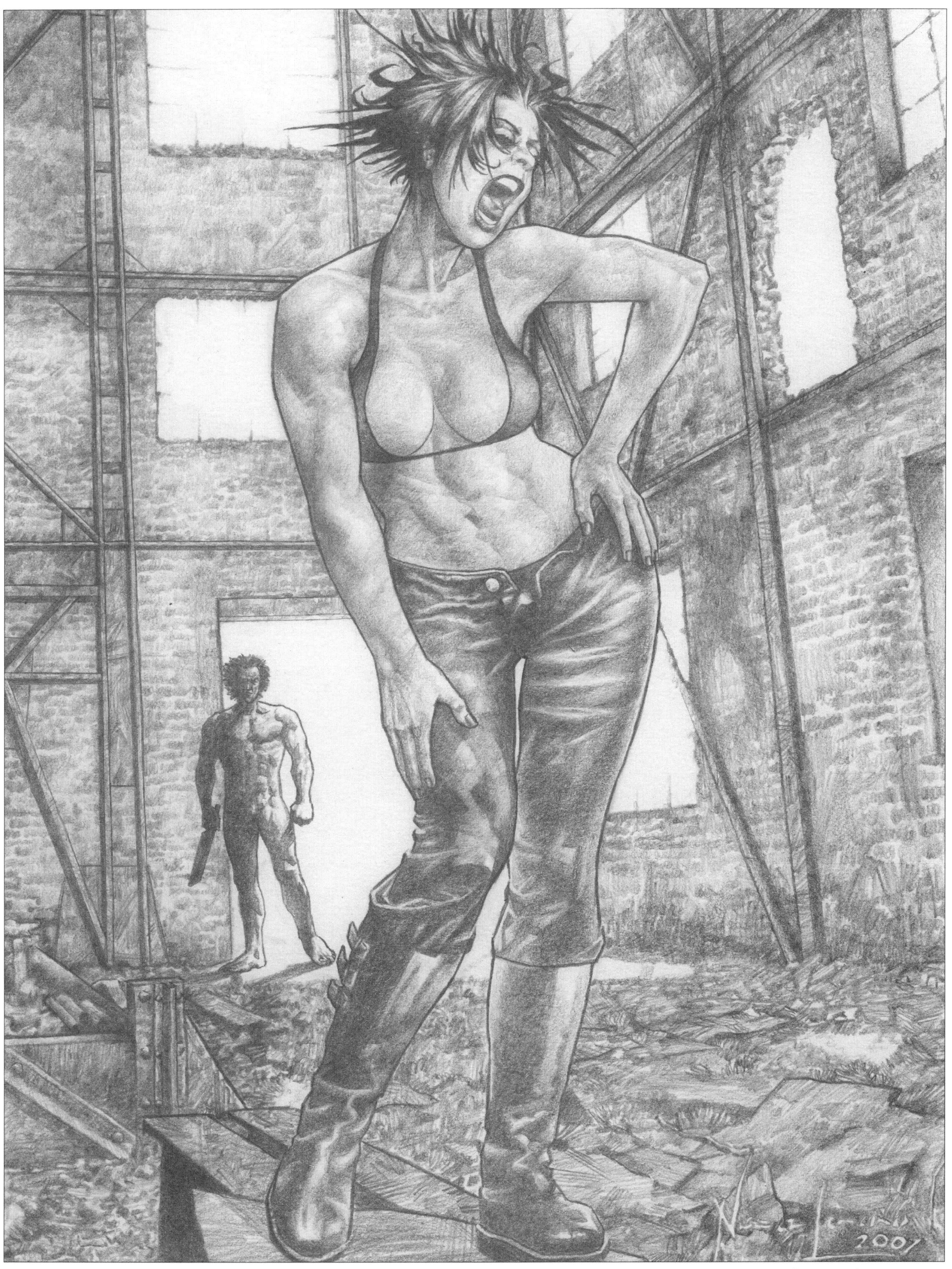

Juan Lencina

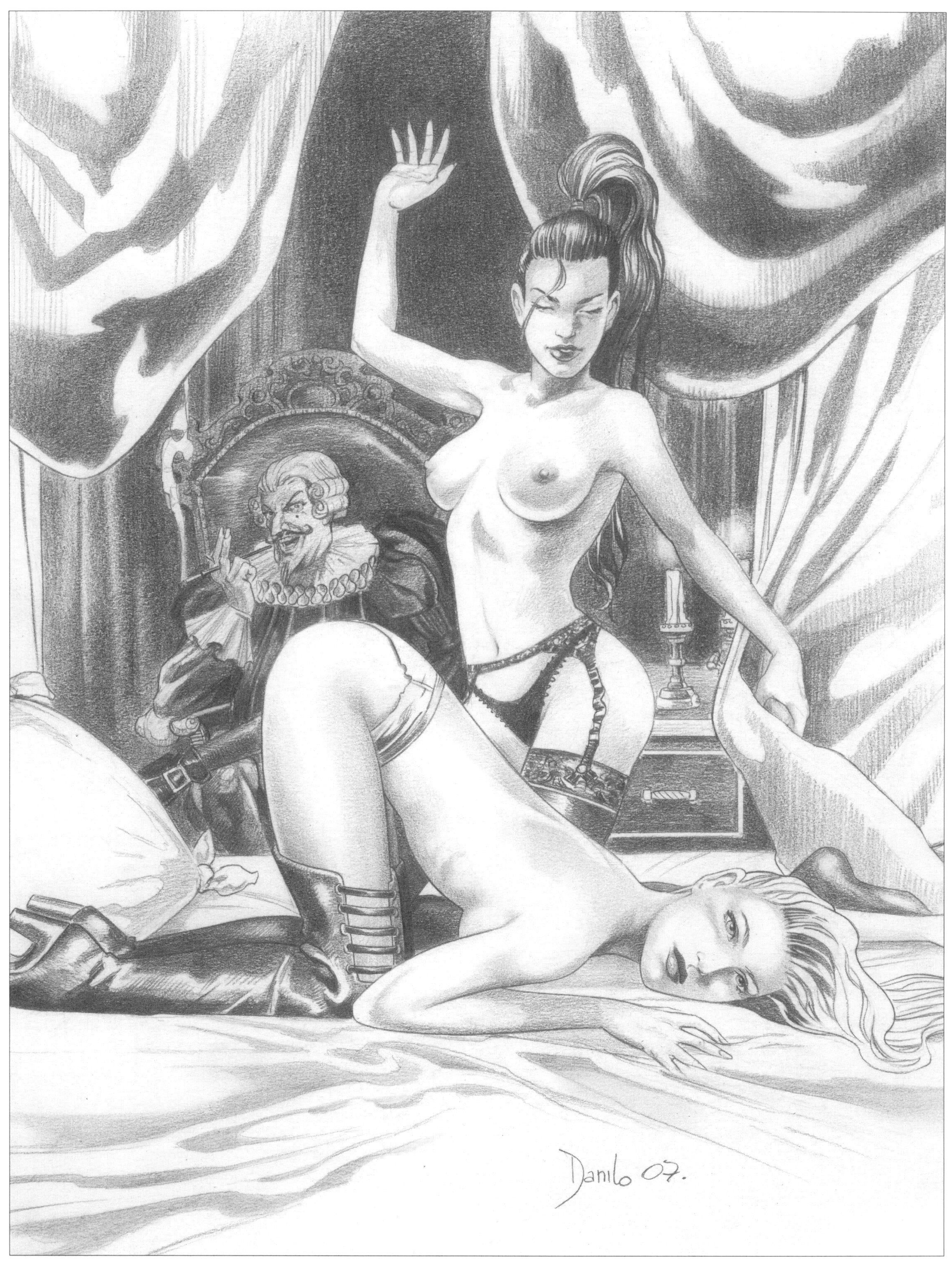

Danilo Guida

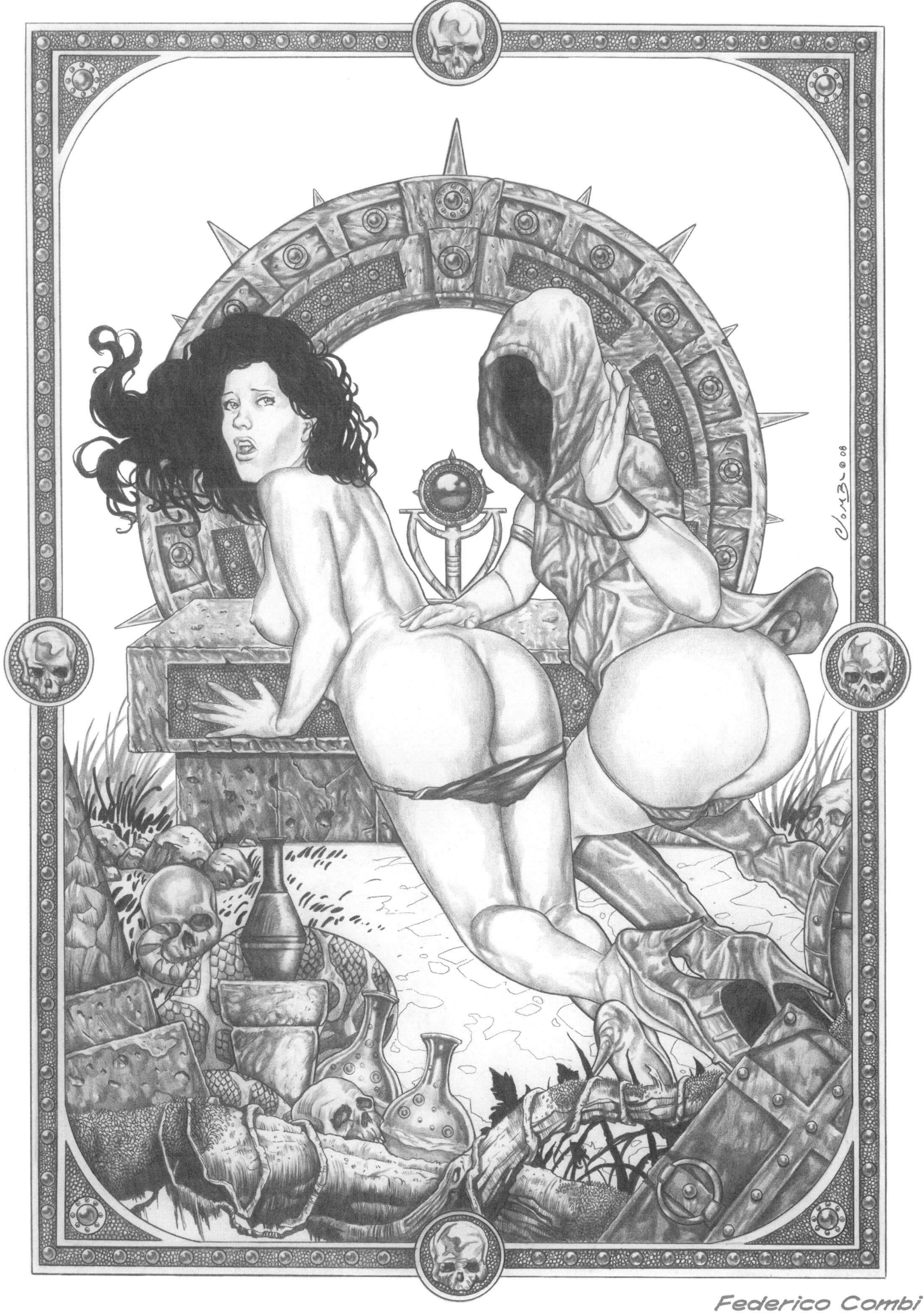

Federico Combi

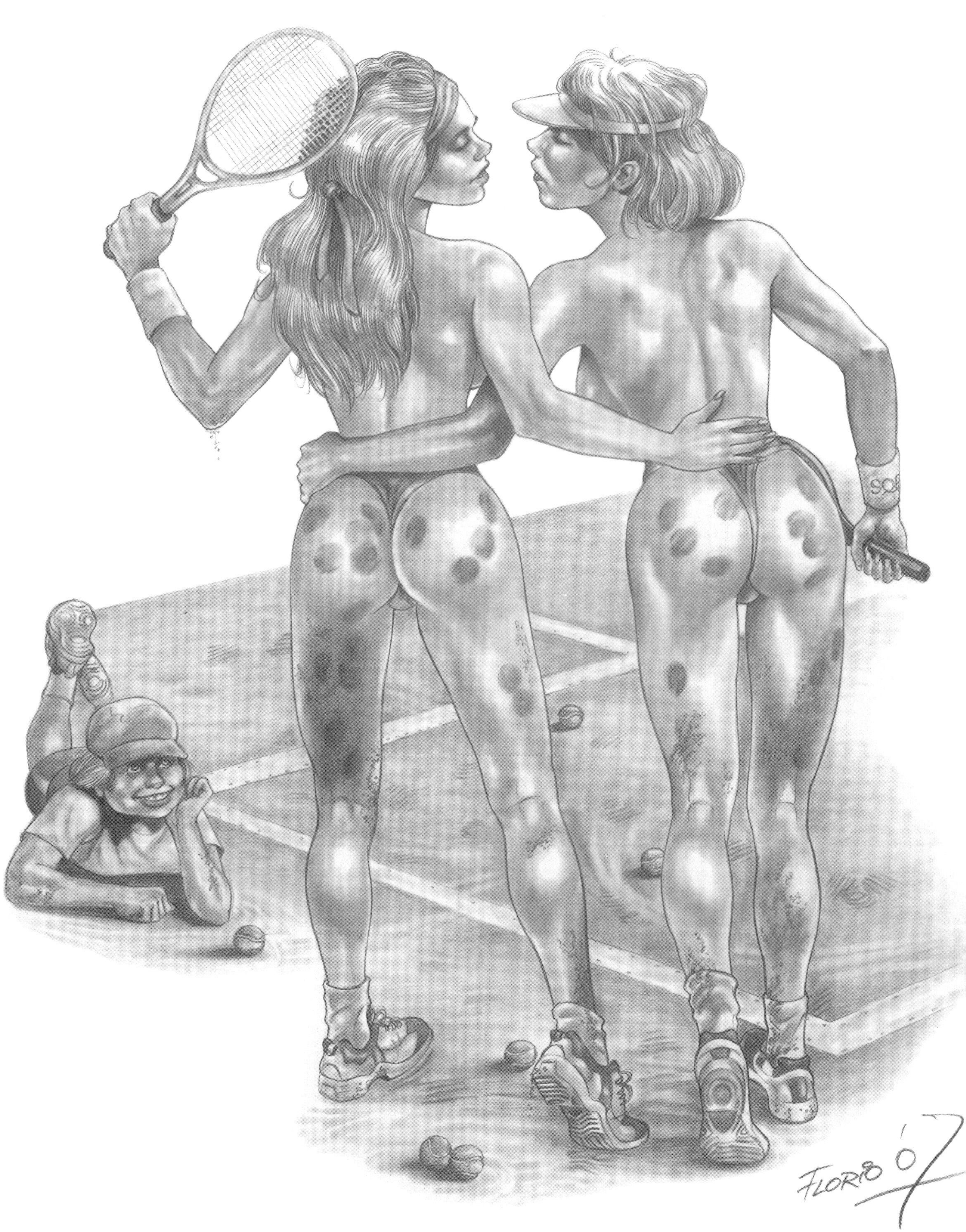

Diego Florio

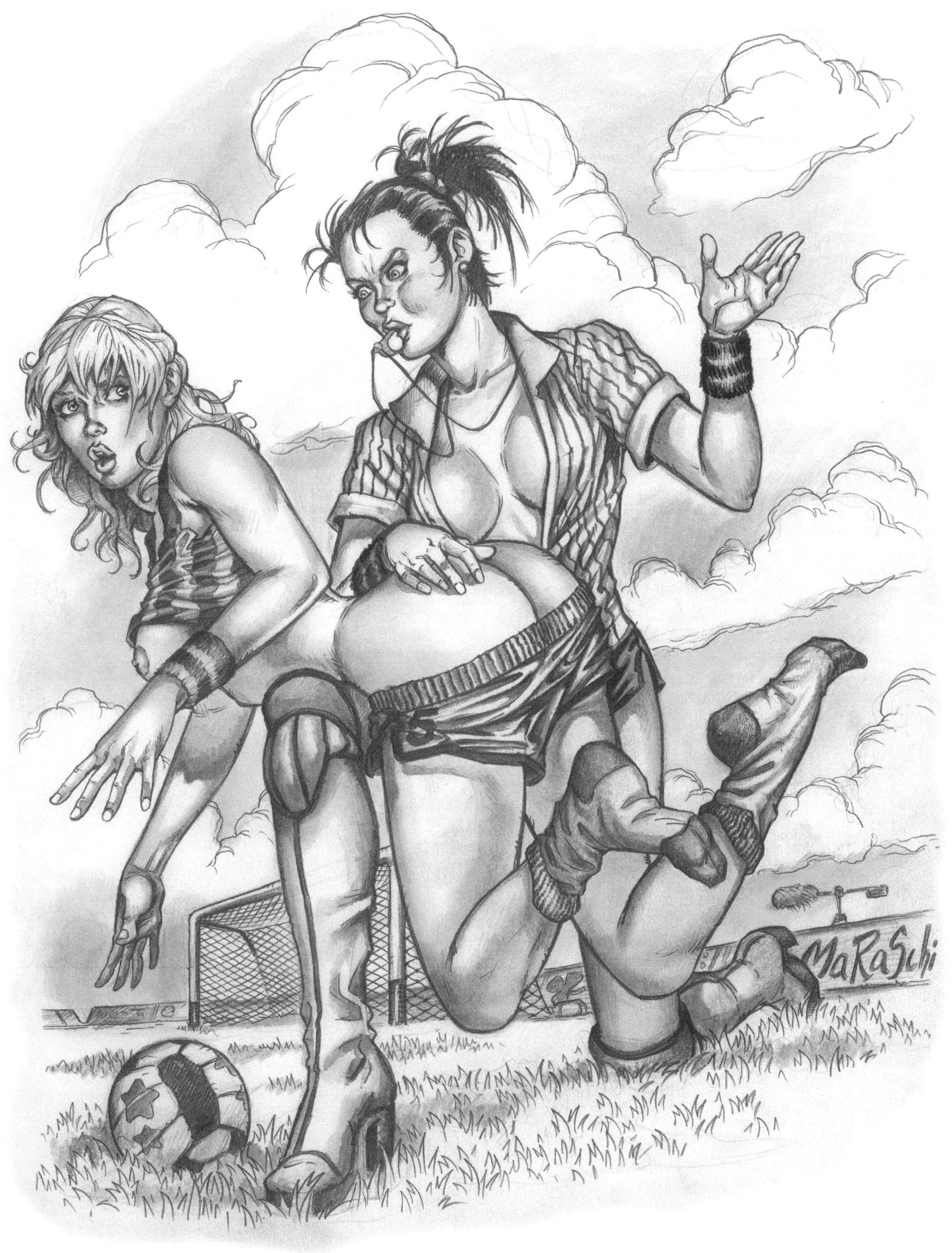

Anibal Maraschi

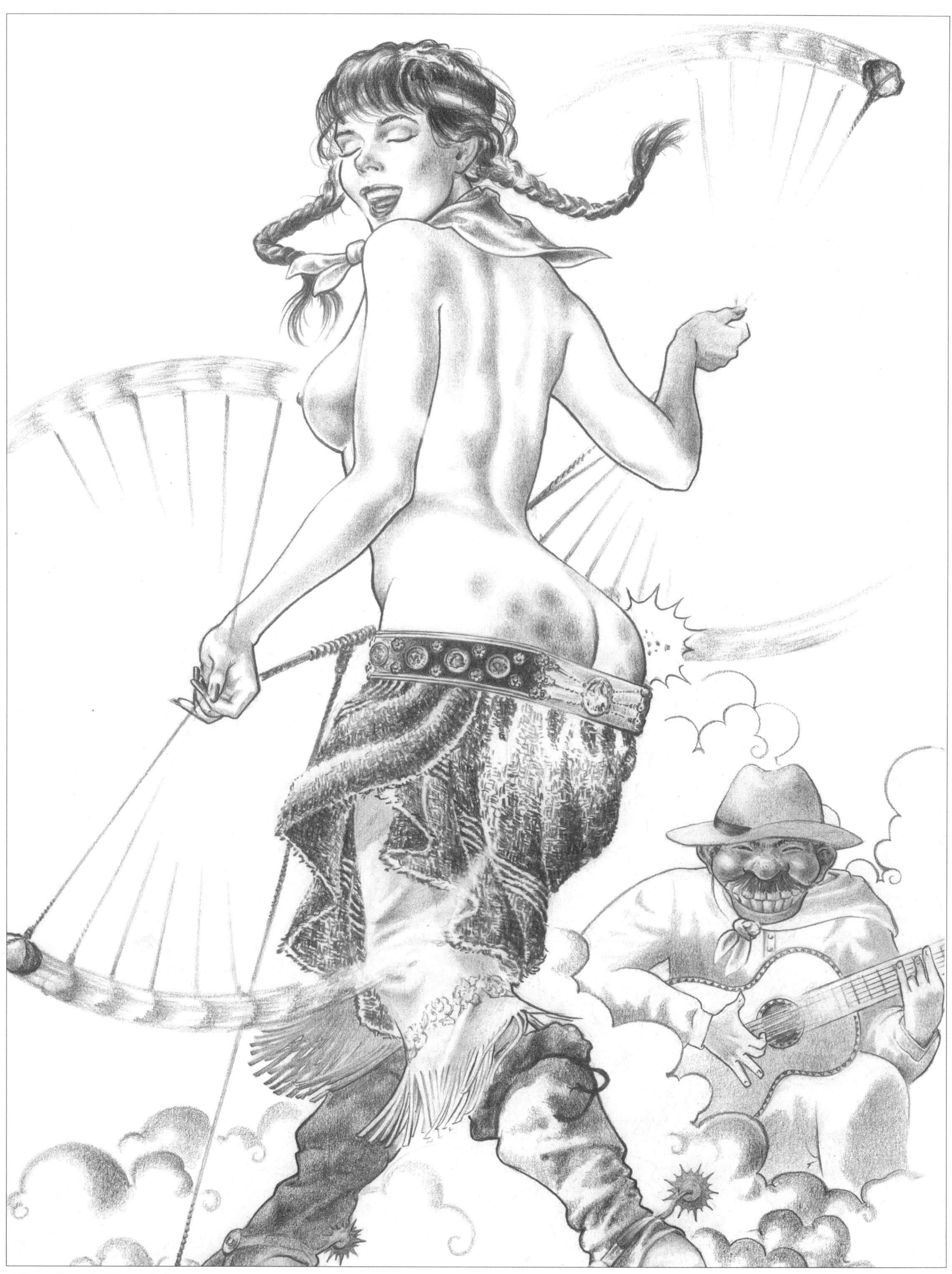

Perla Pilucki

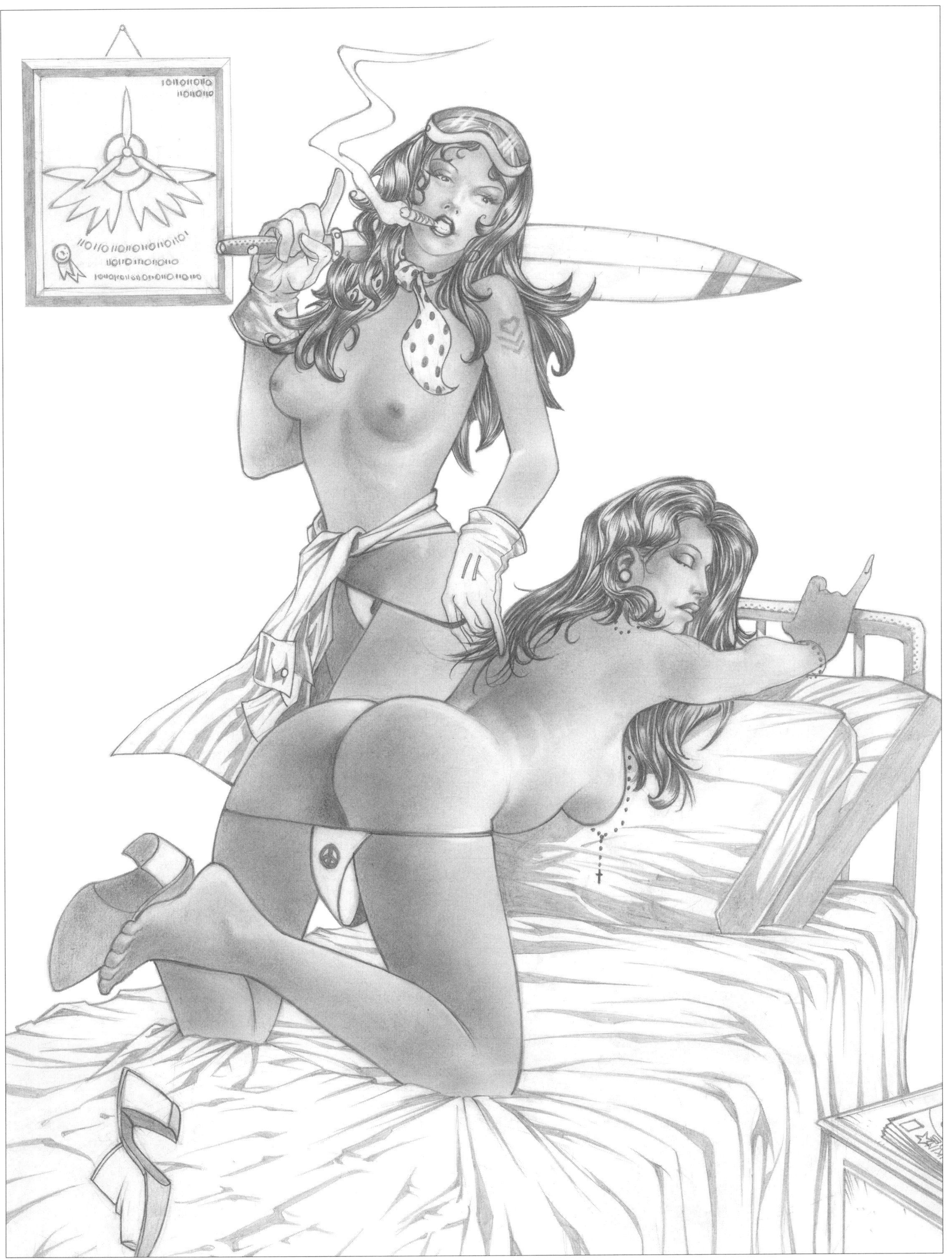

J.L. Czerniawski

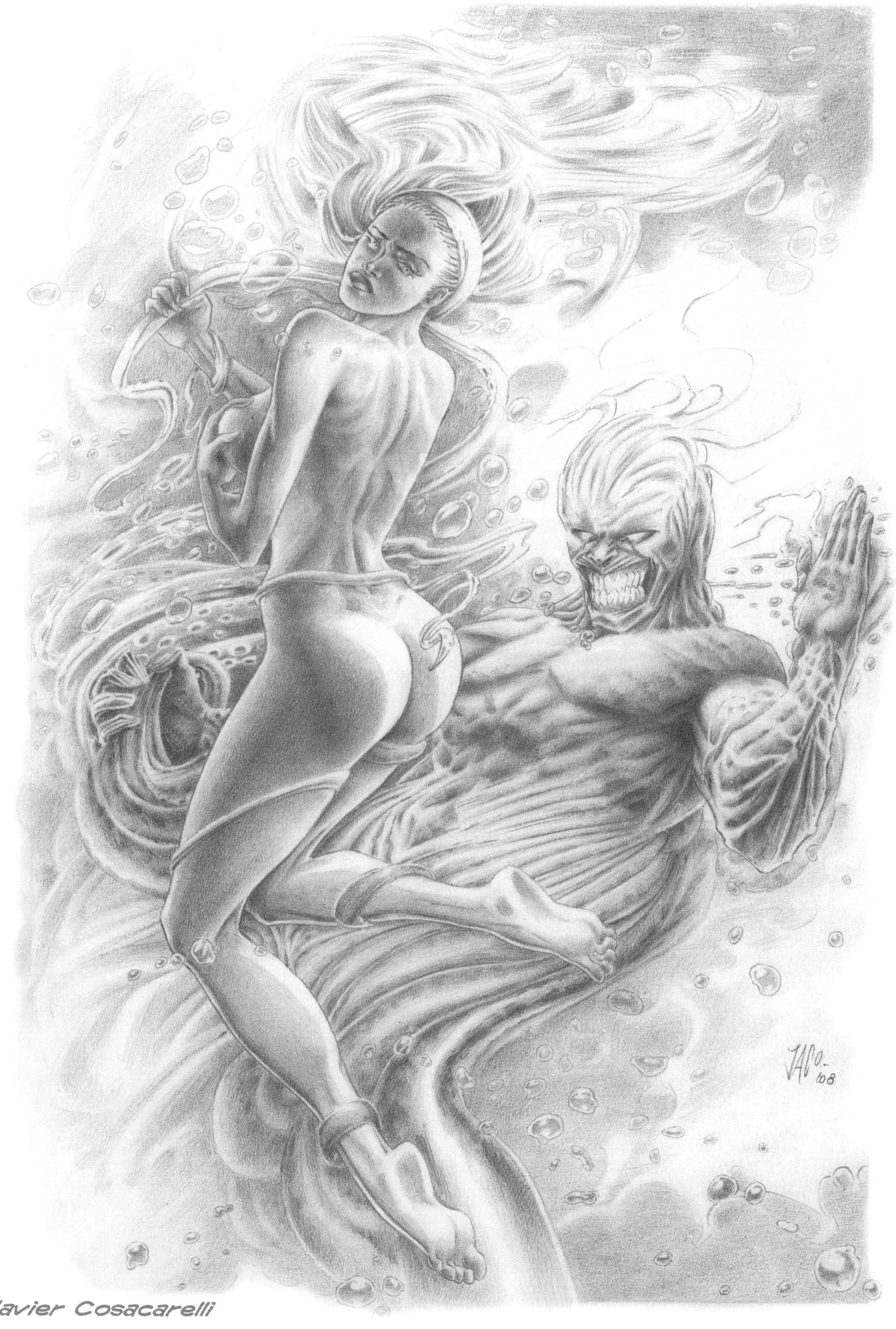

Javier Cosacarelli

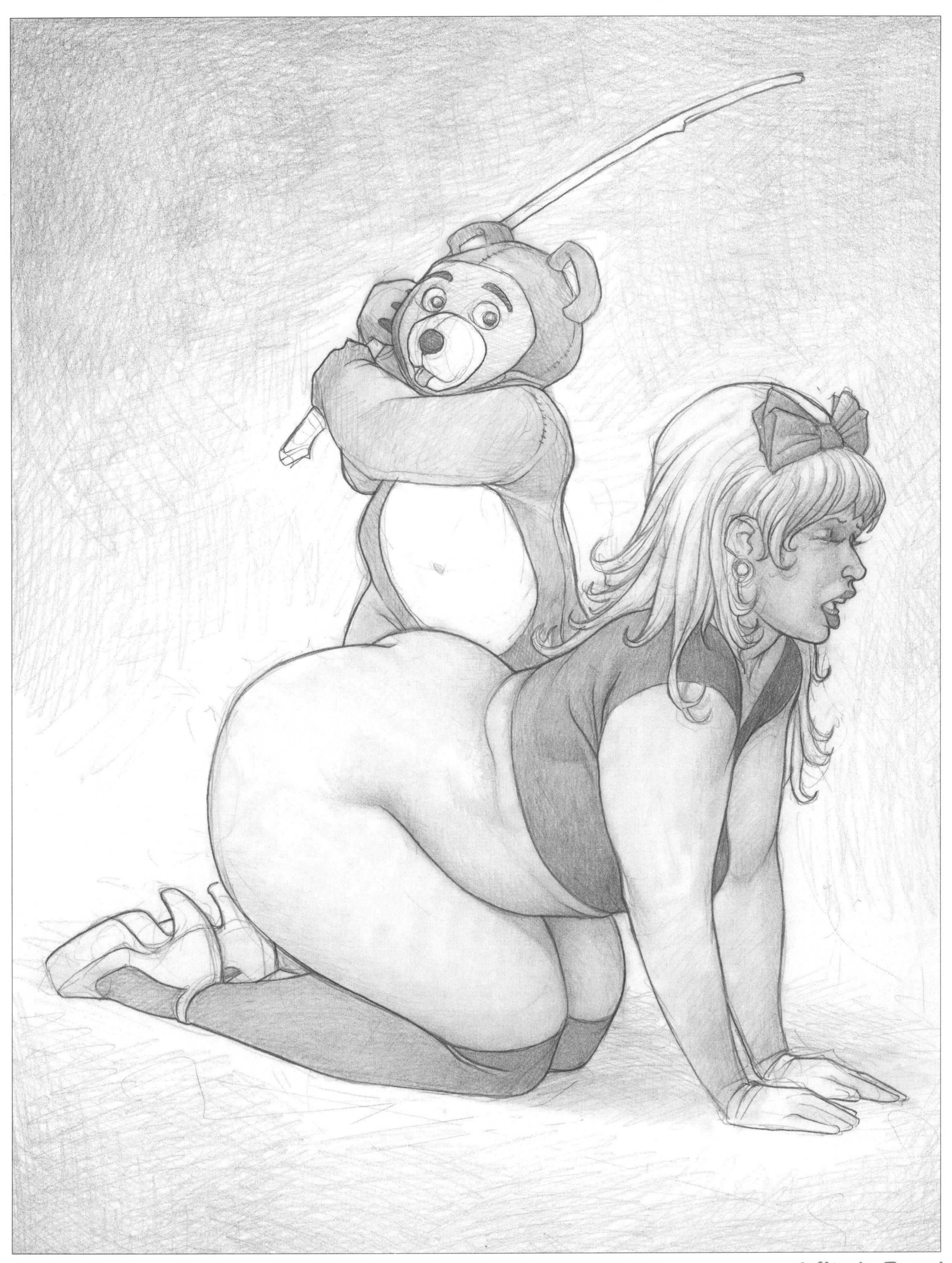

Mitch Byrd

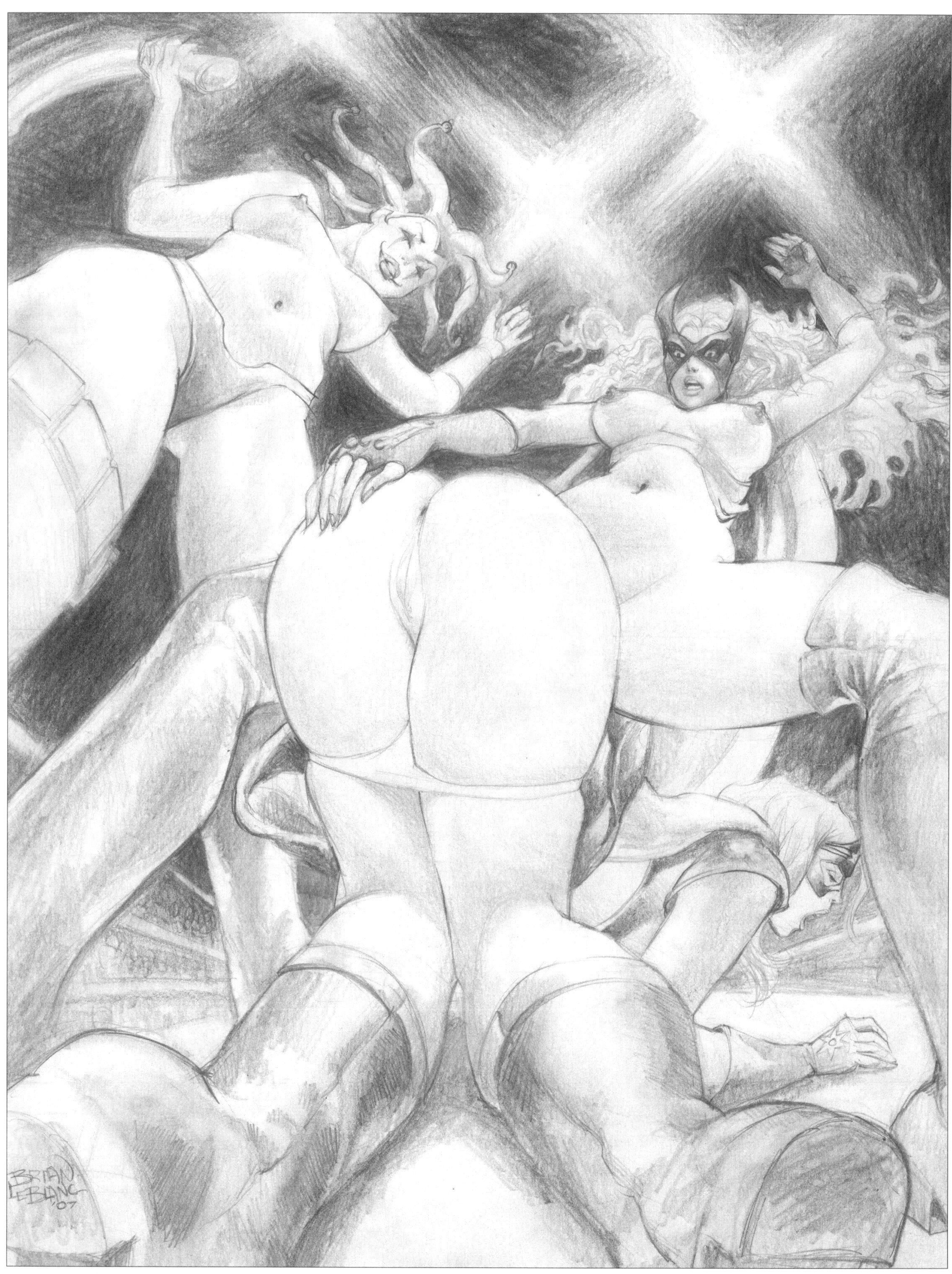

Brian LeBlanc

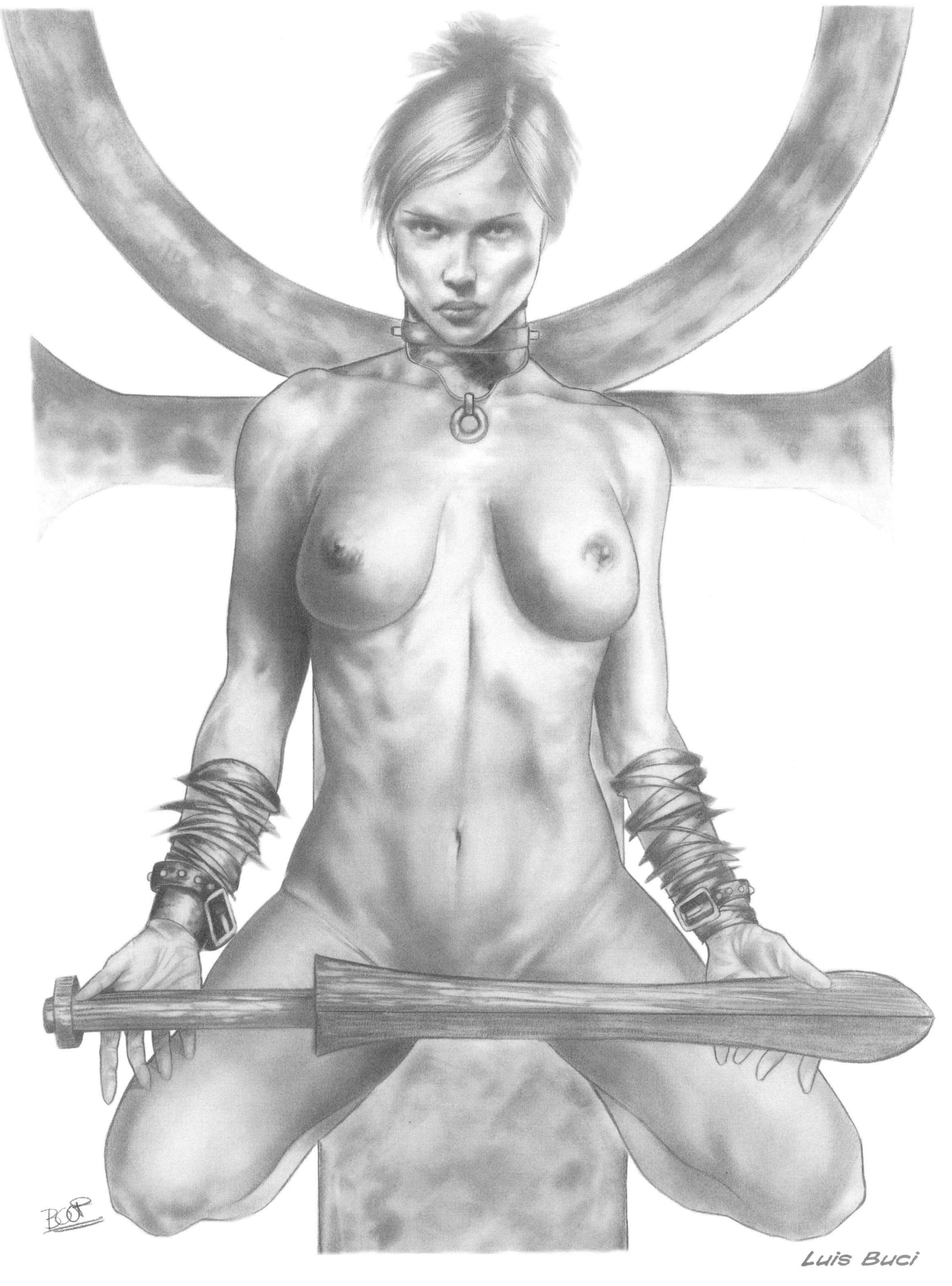

Luis Buci

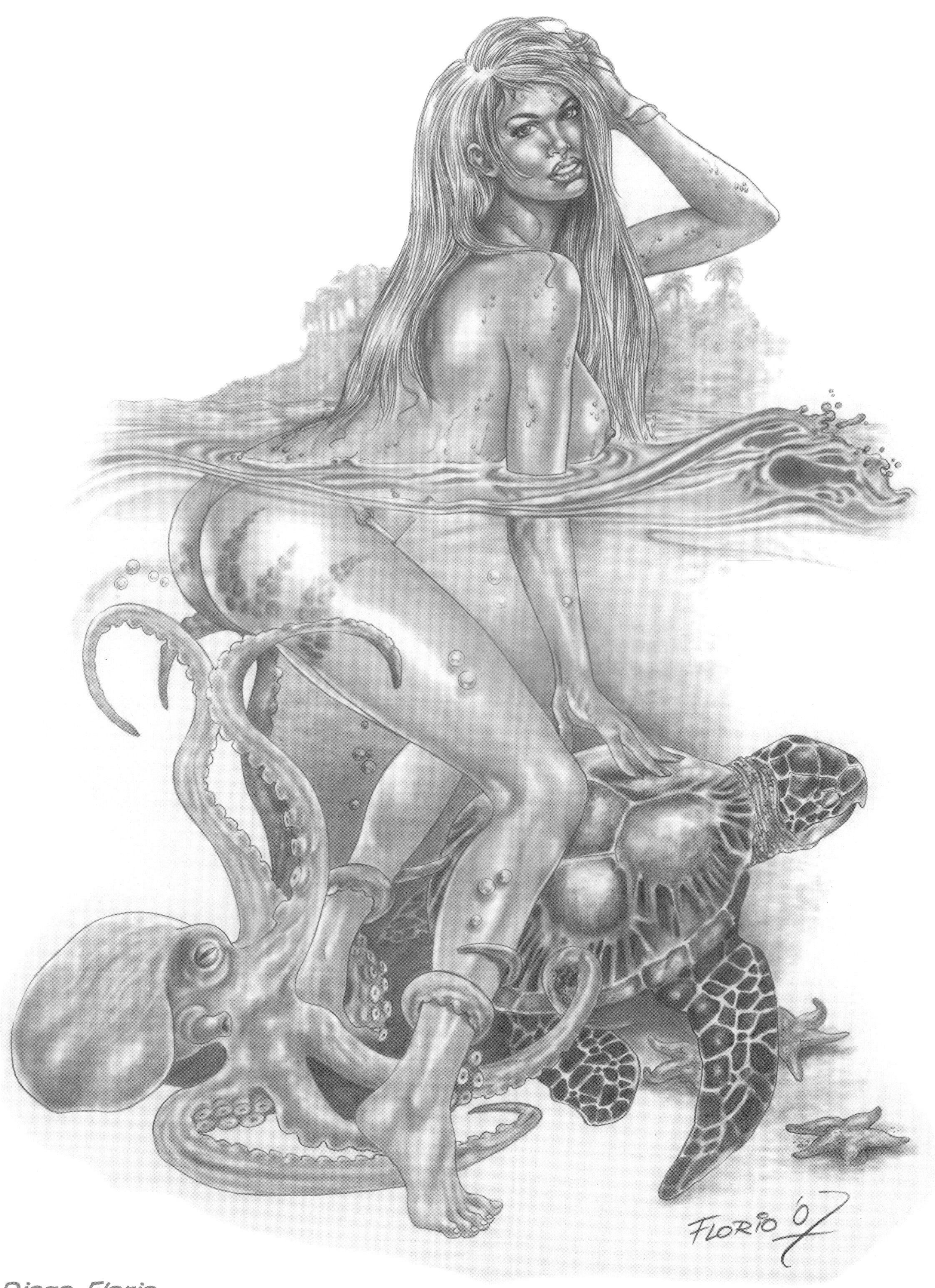

Diego Florio

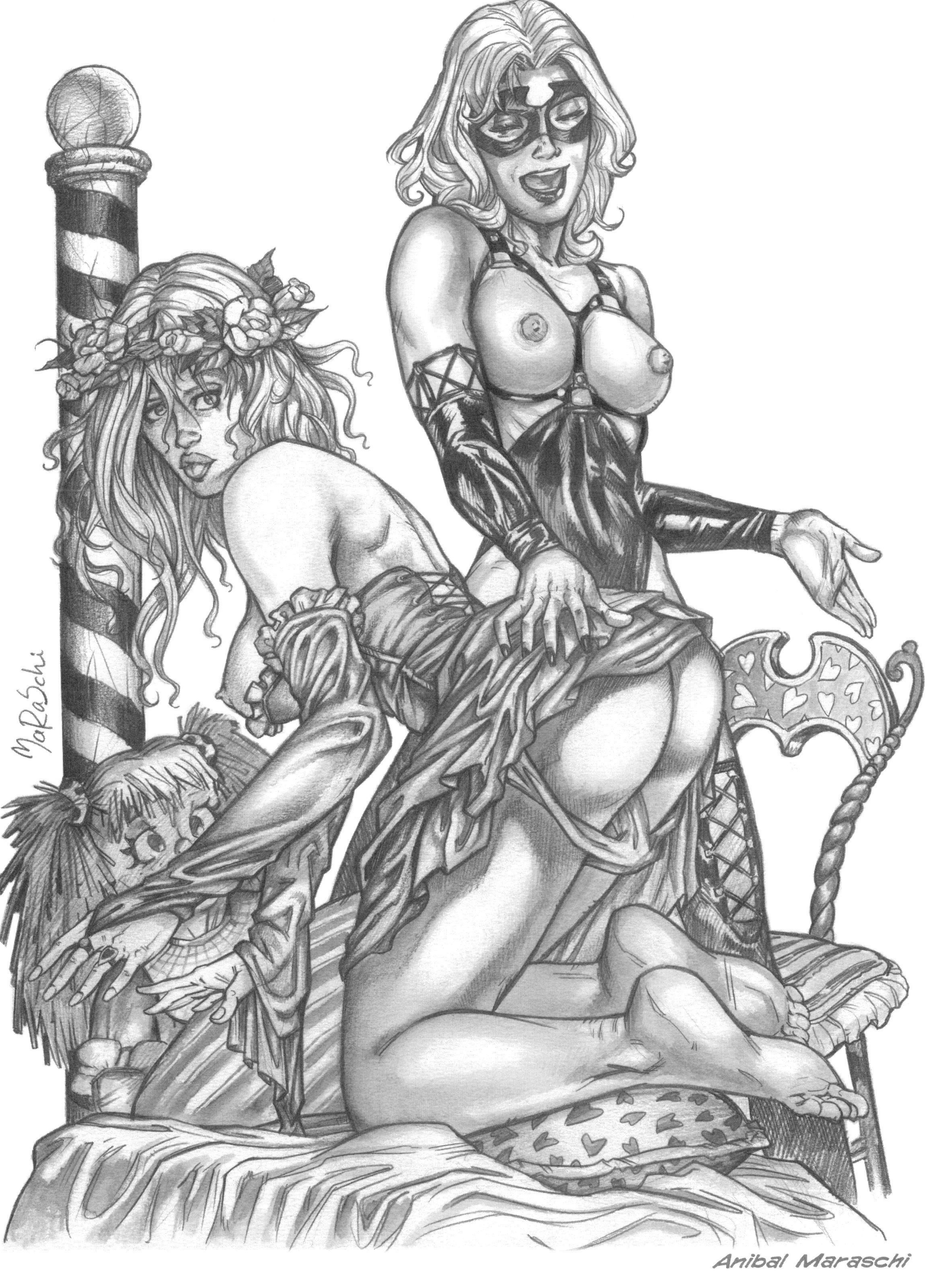

Anibal Maraschi

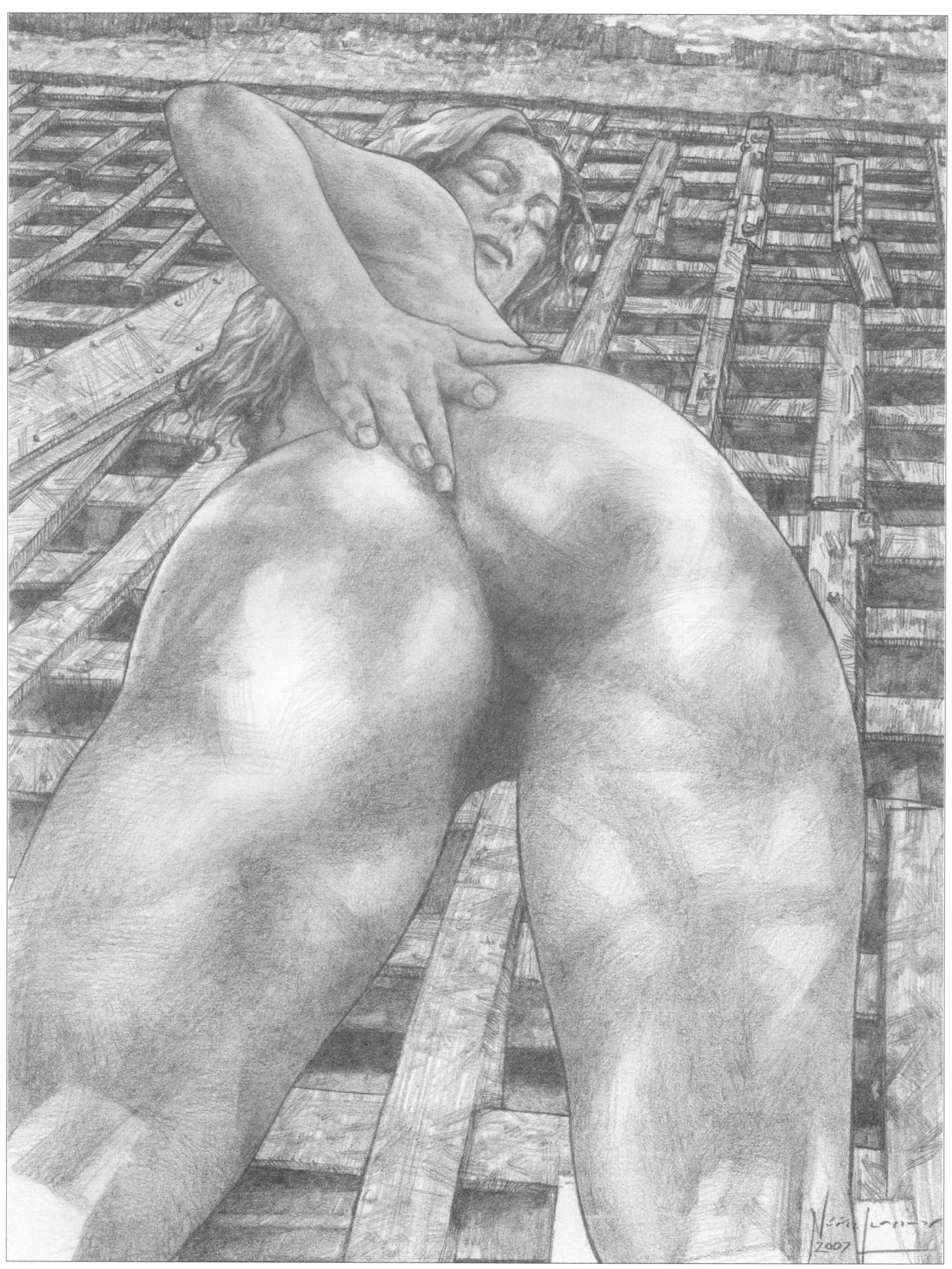

Juan Lencina

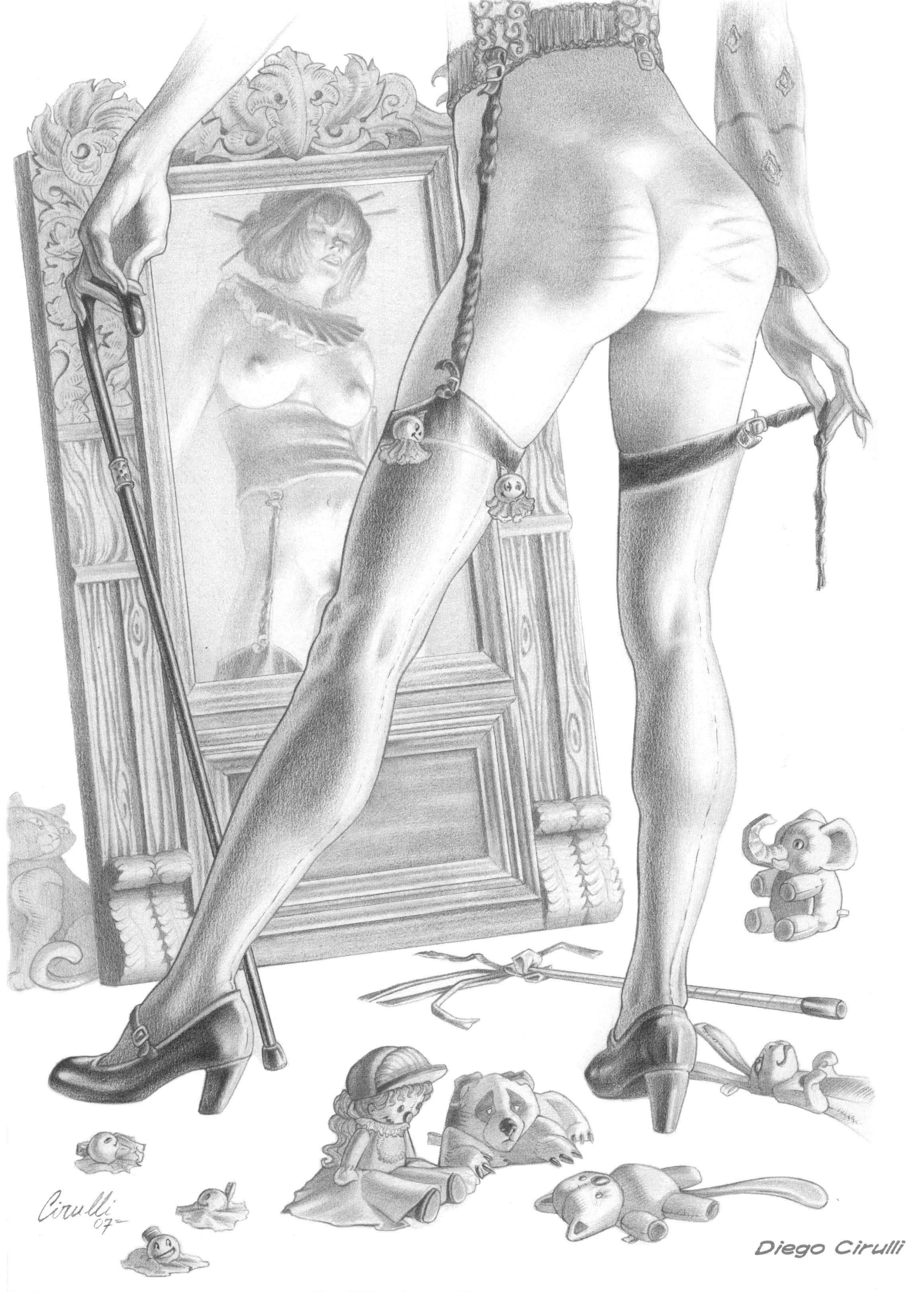

Diego Cirulli

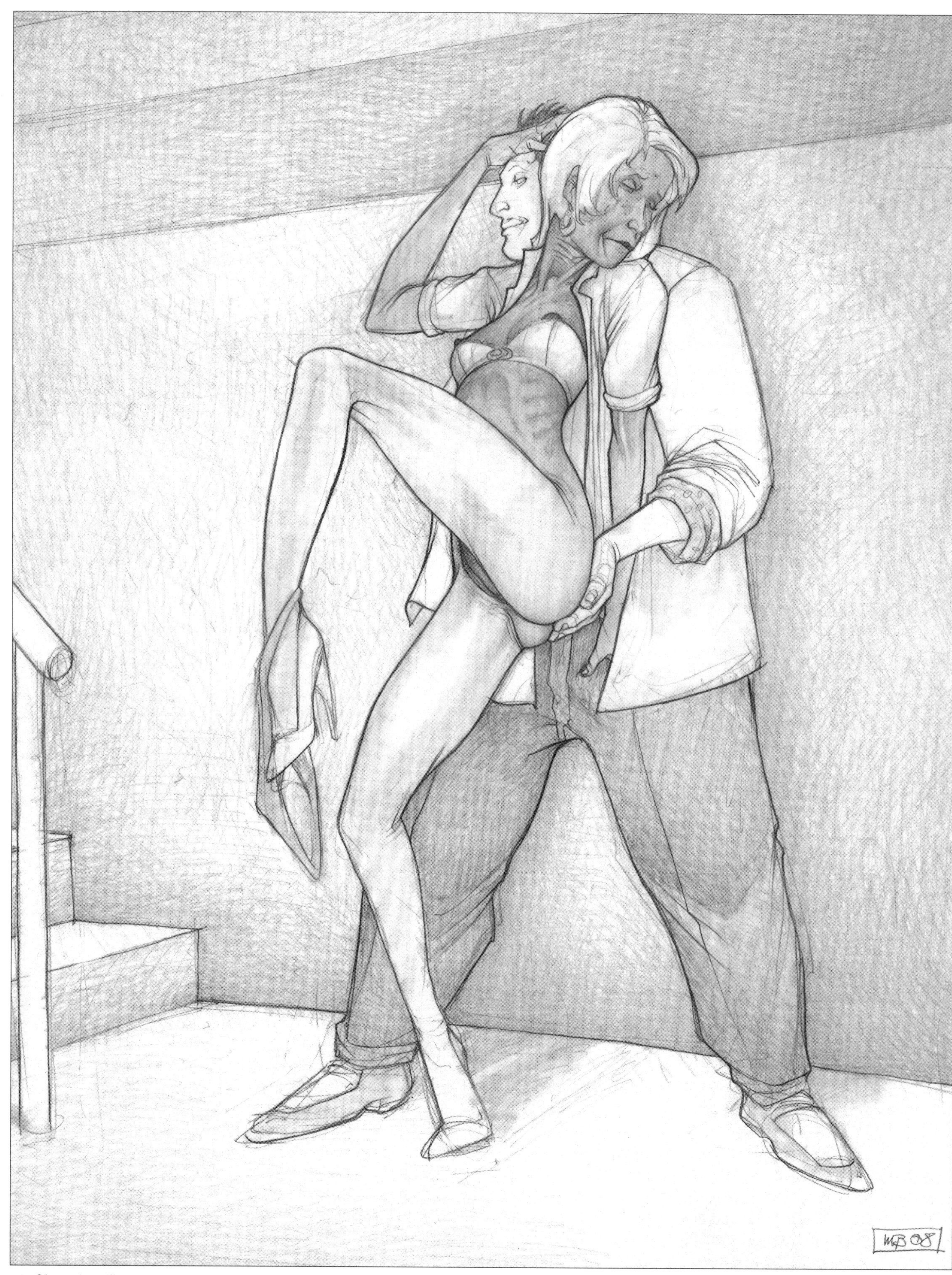

Mitch Byrd

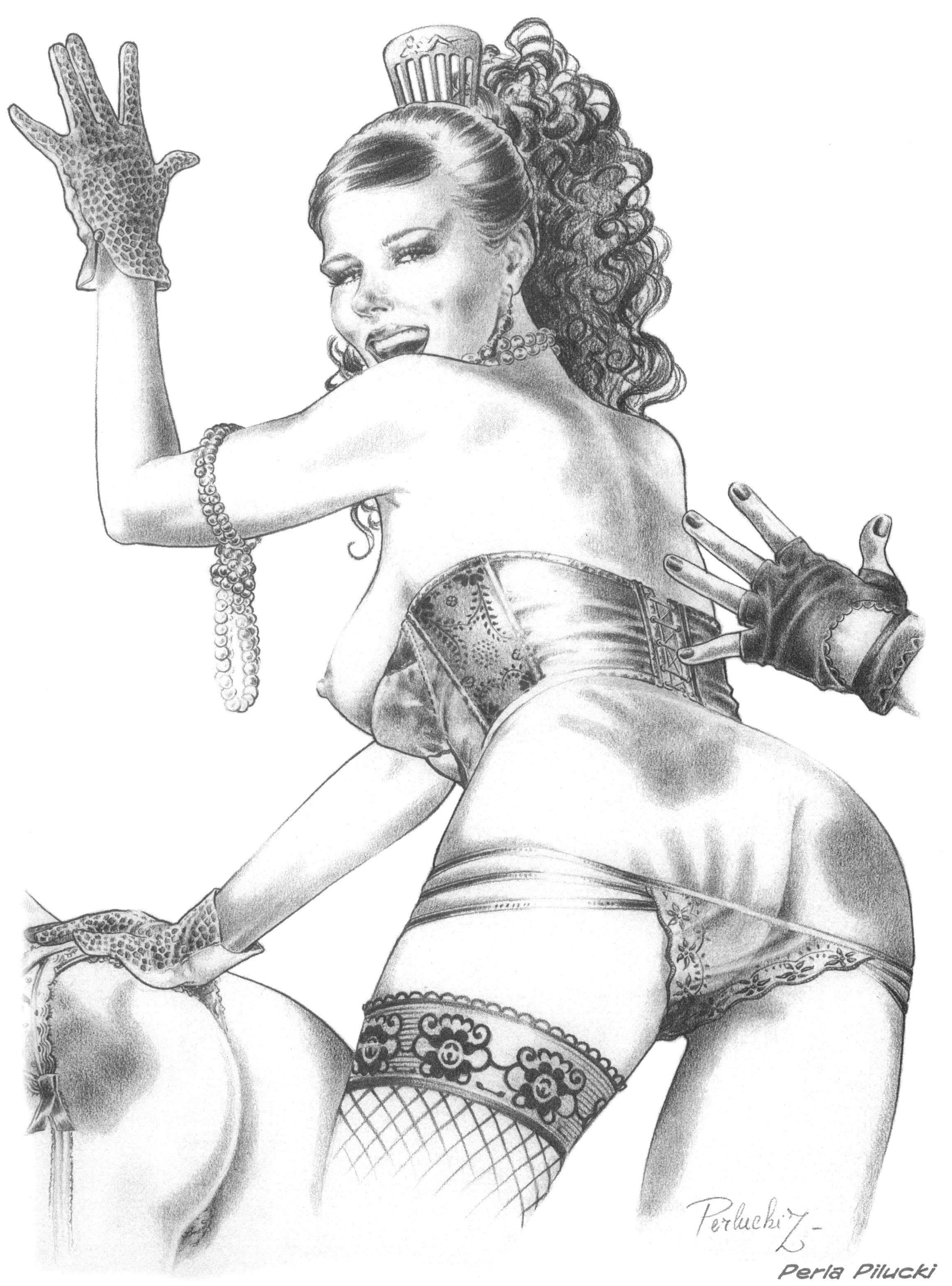

Perla Pilucki

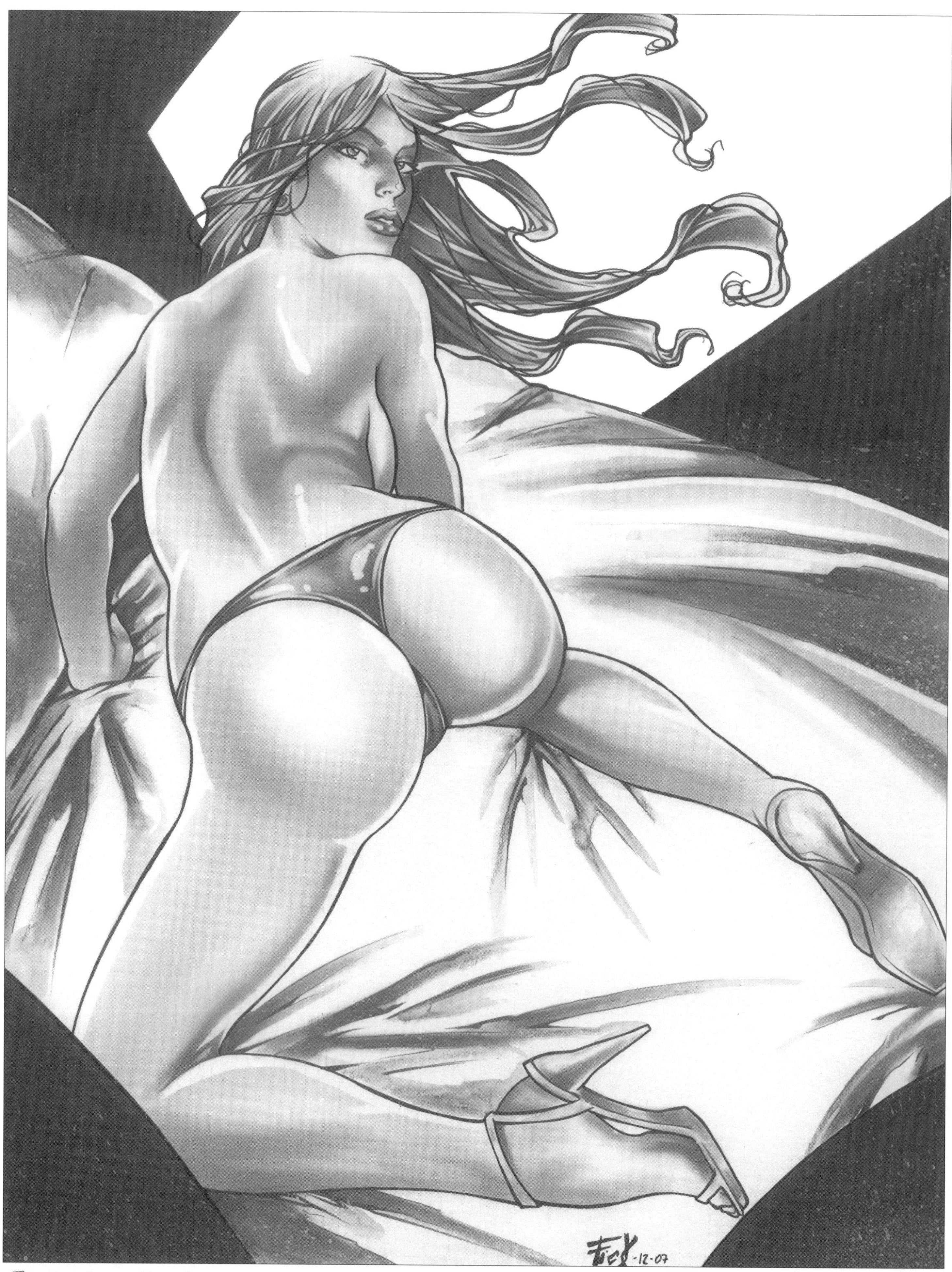

Federico Ossio

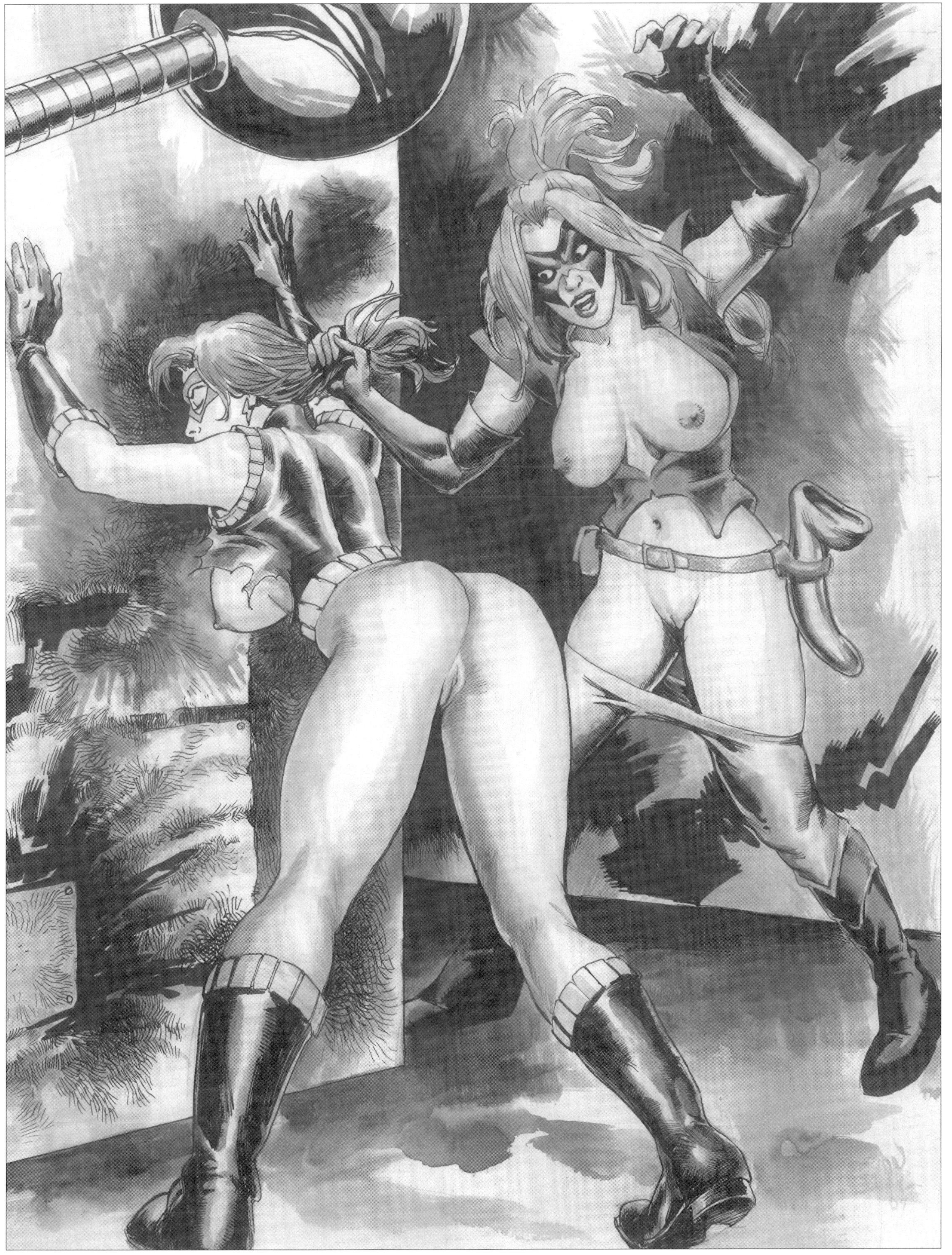

Brian LeBlanc

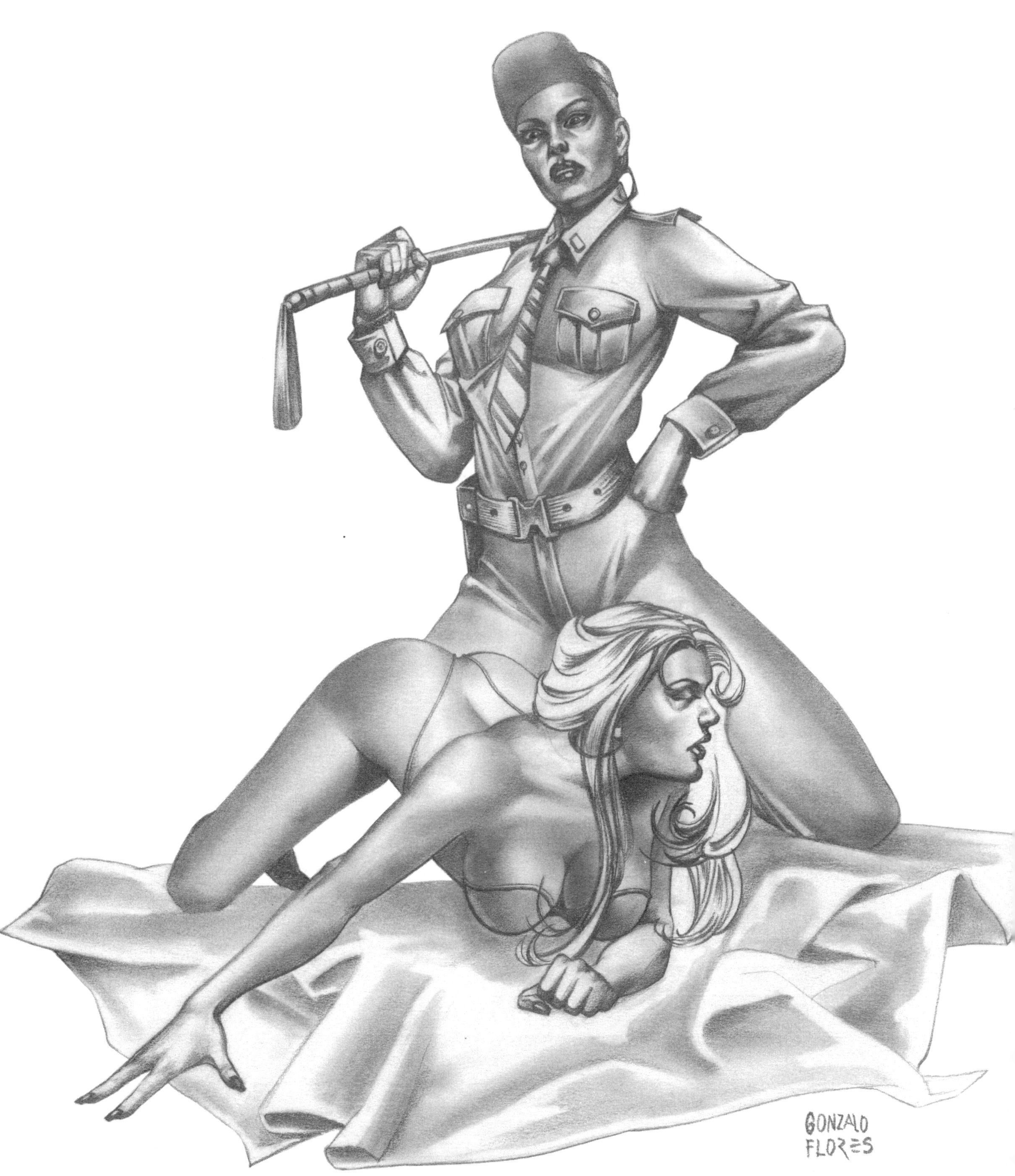

Gonzalo Flores

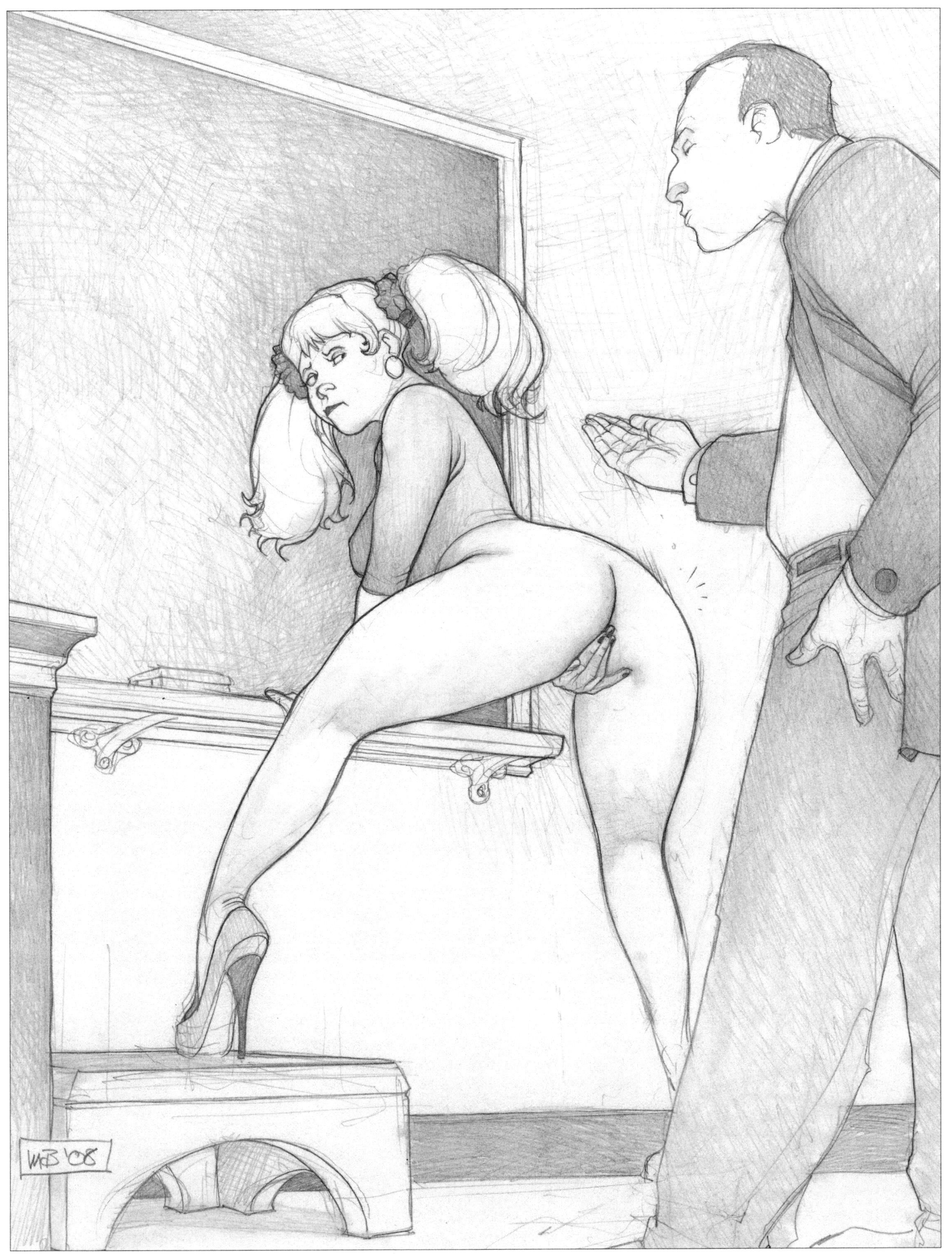

Mitch Byrd

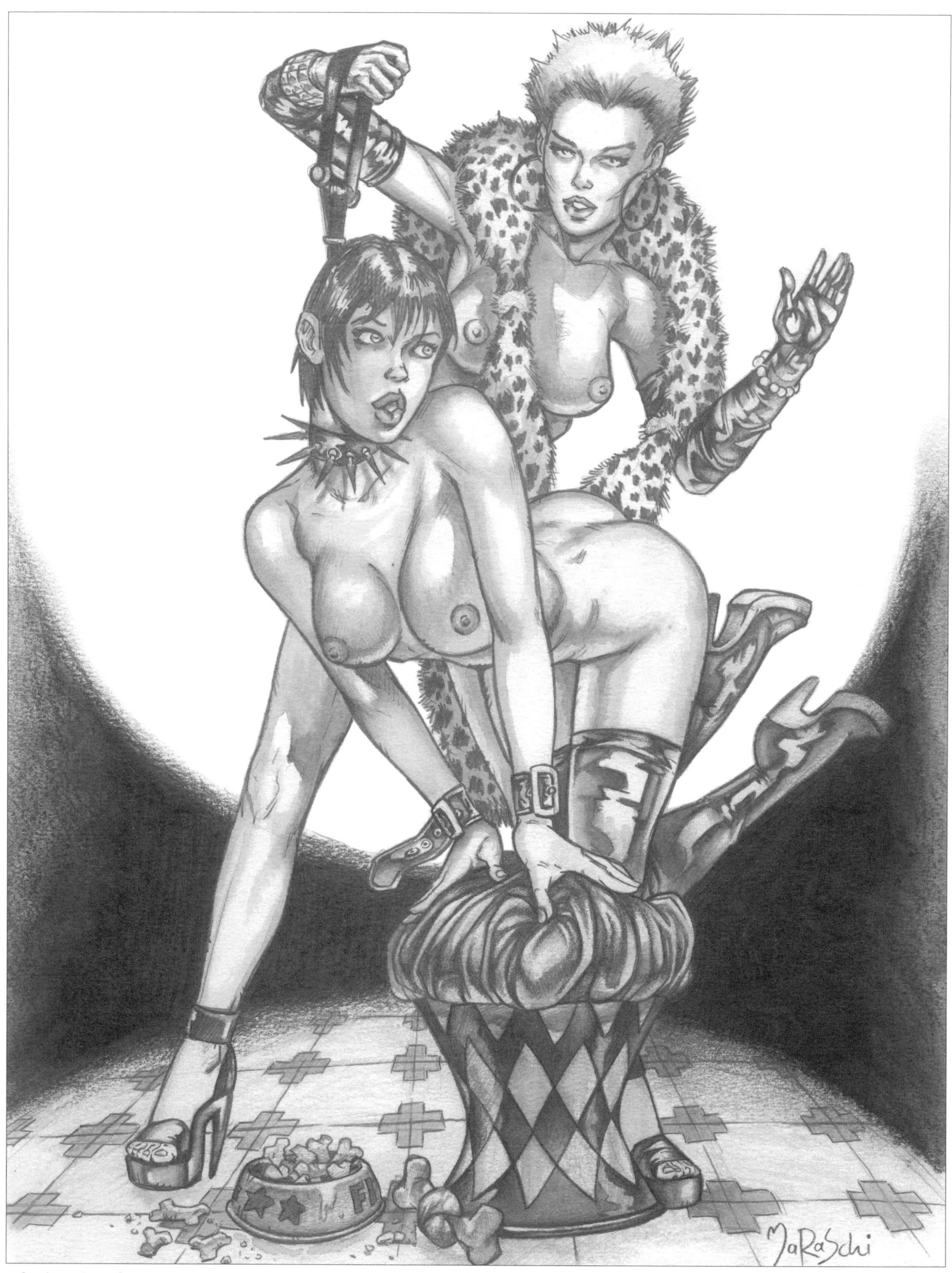

Anibal Maraschi

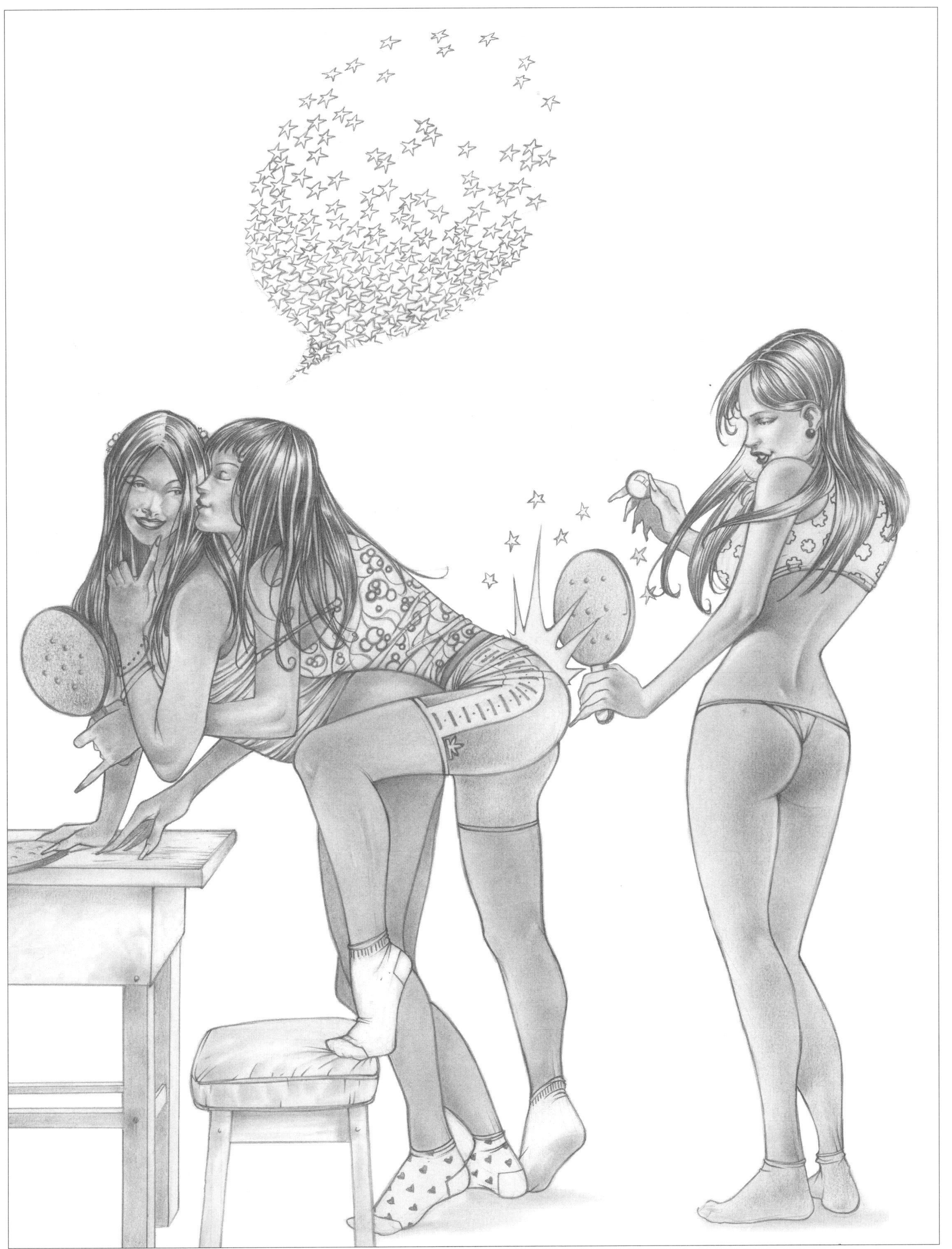

J.L. Czerniawski

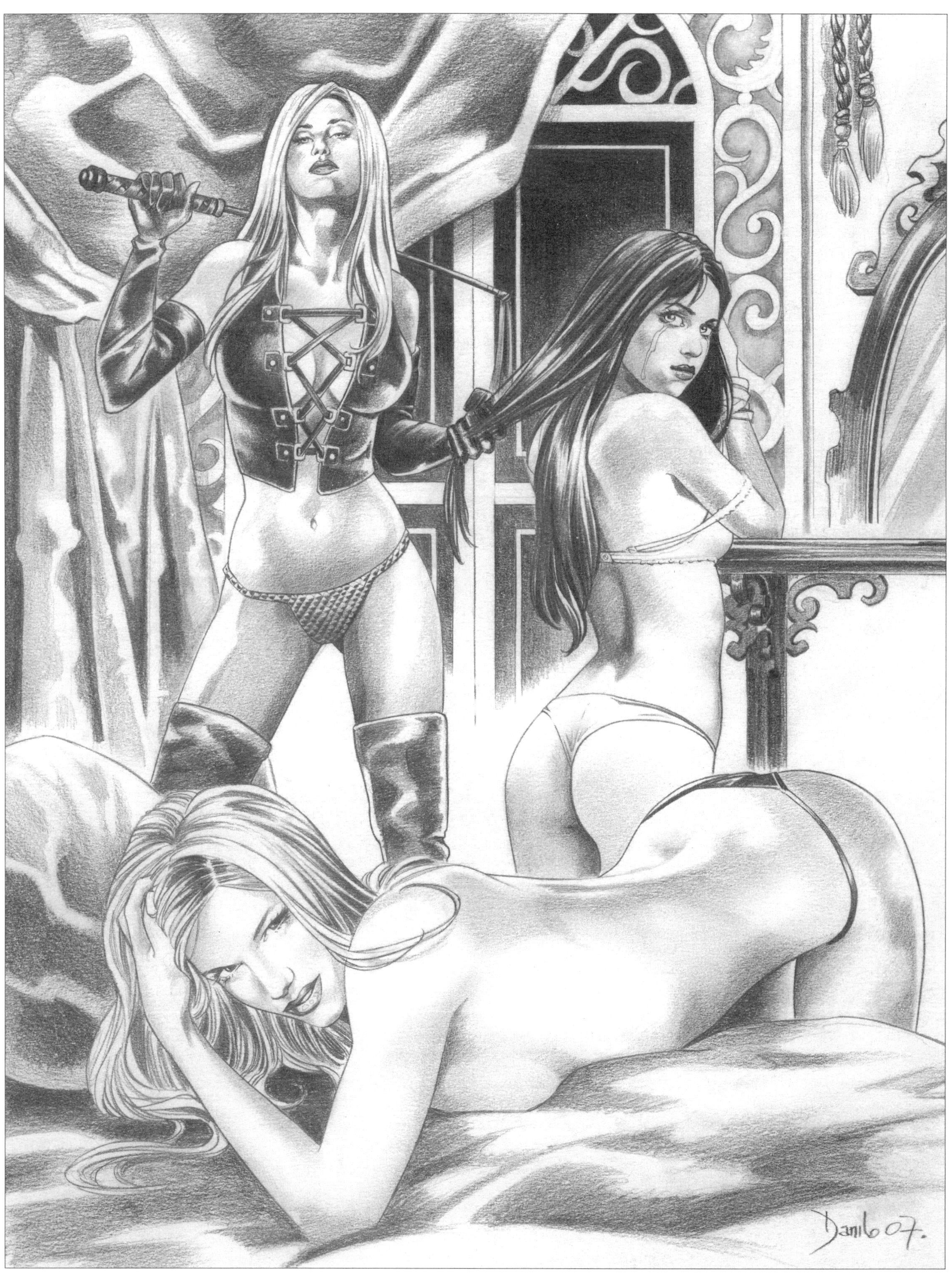

Danilo Guida

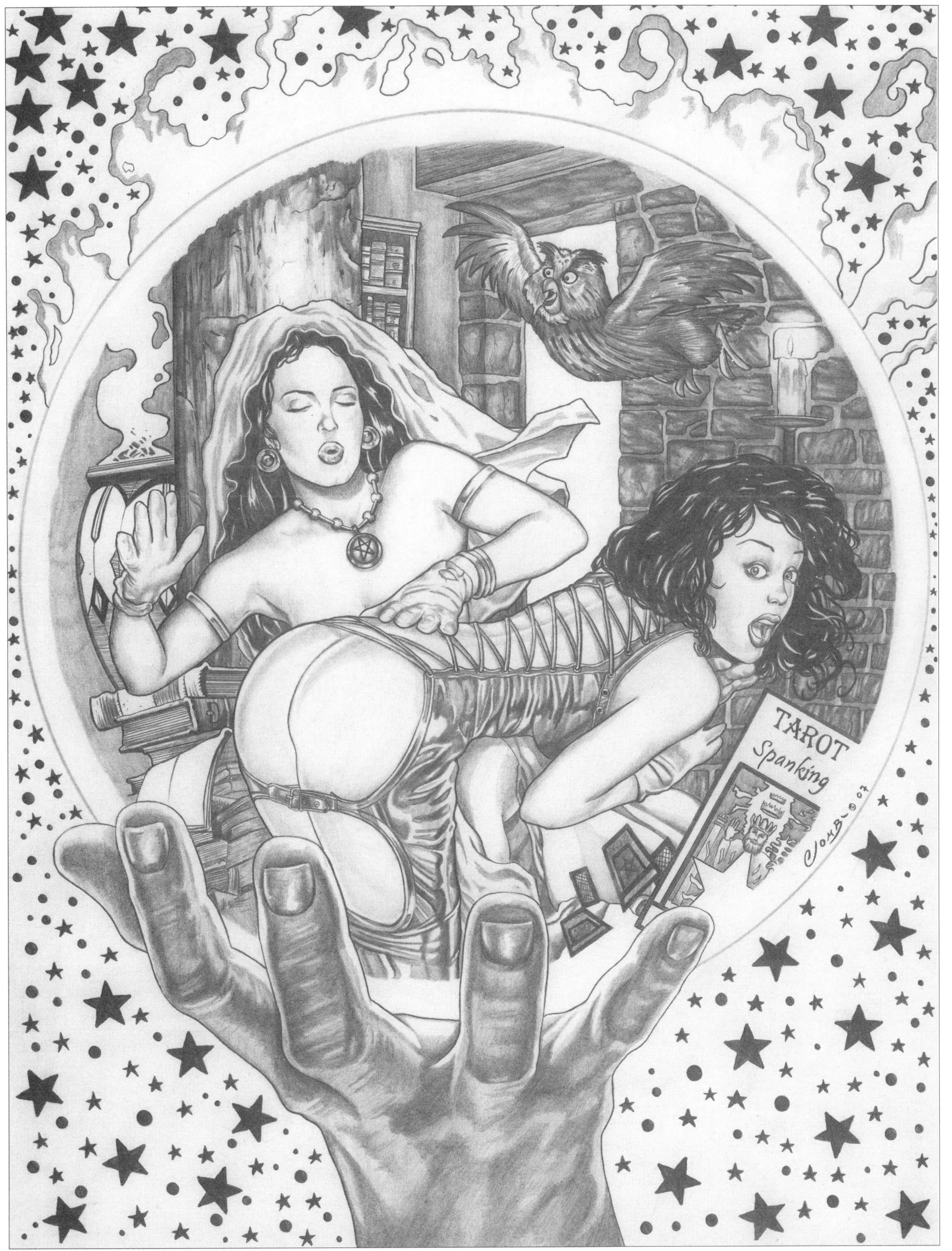

Federico Combi

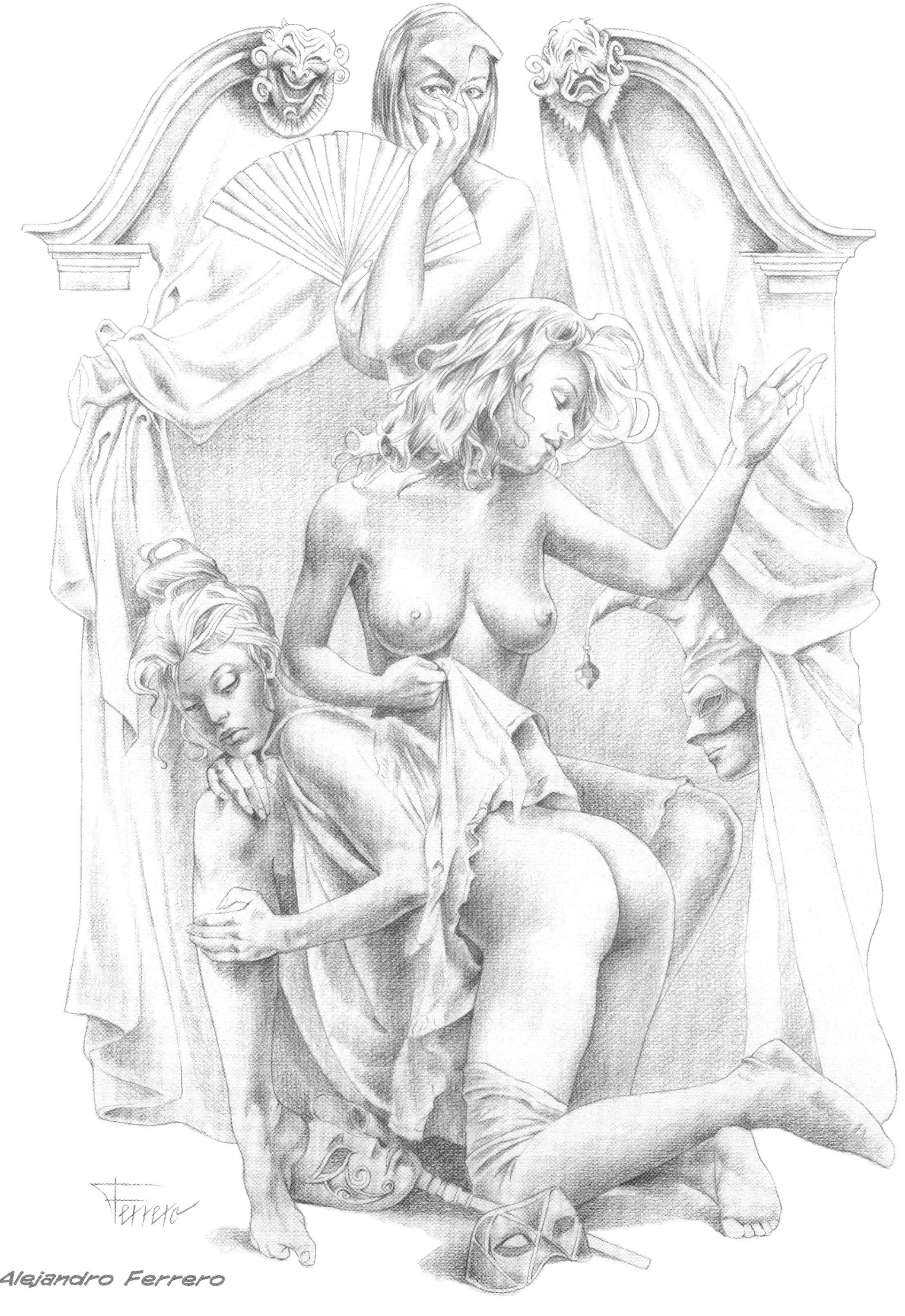

Alejandro Ferrero

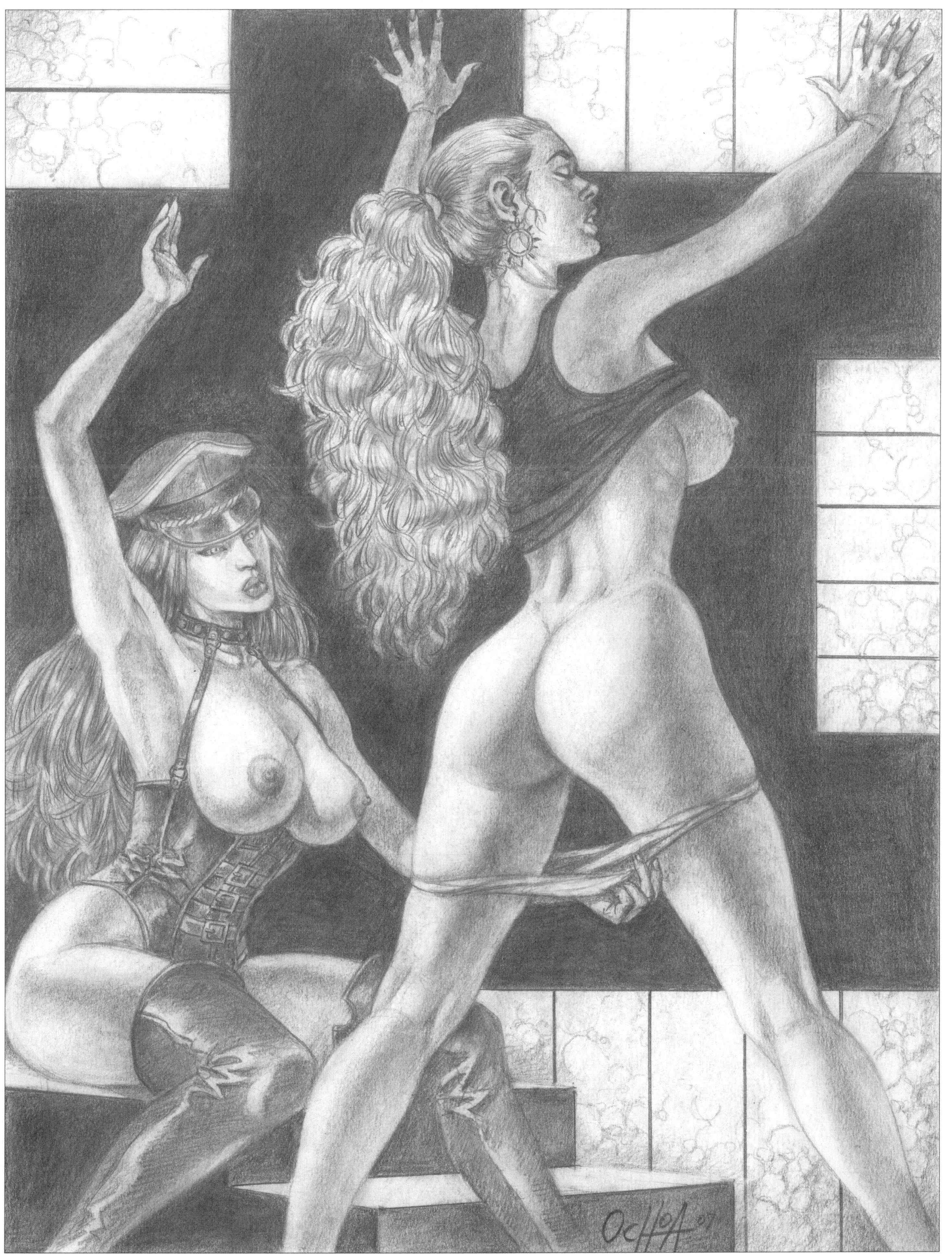

Percy Ochoa

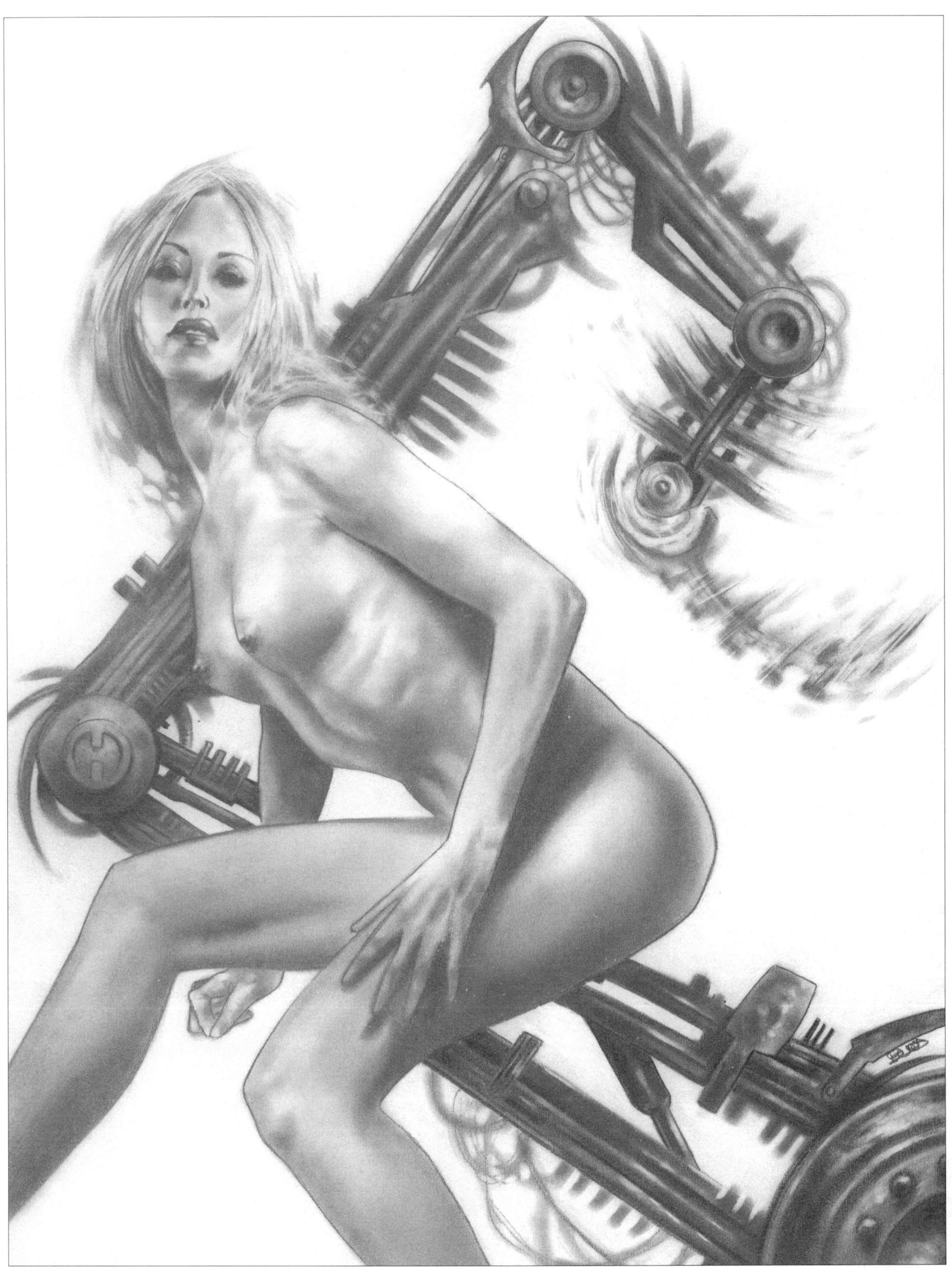

Luis Buci

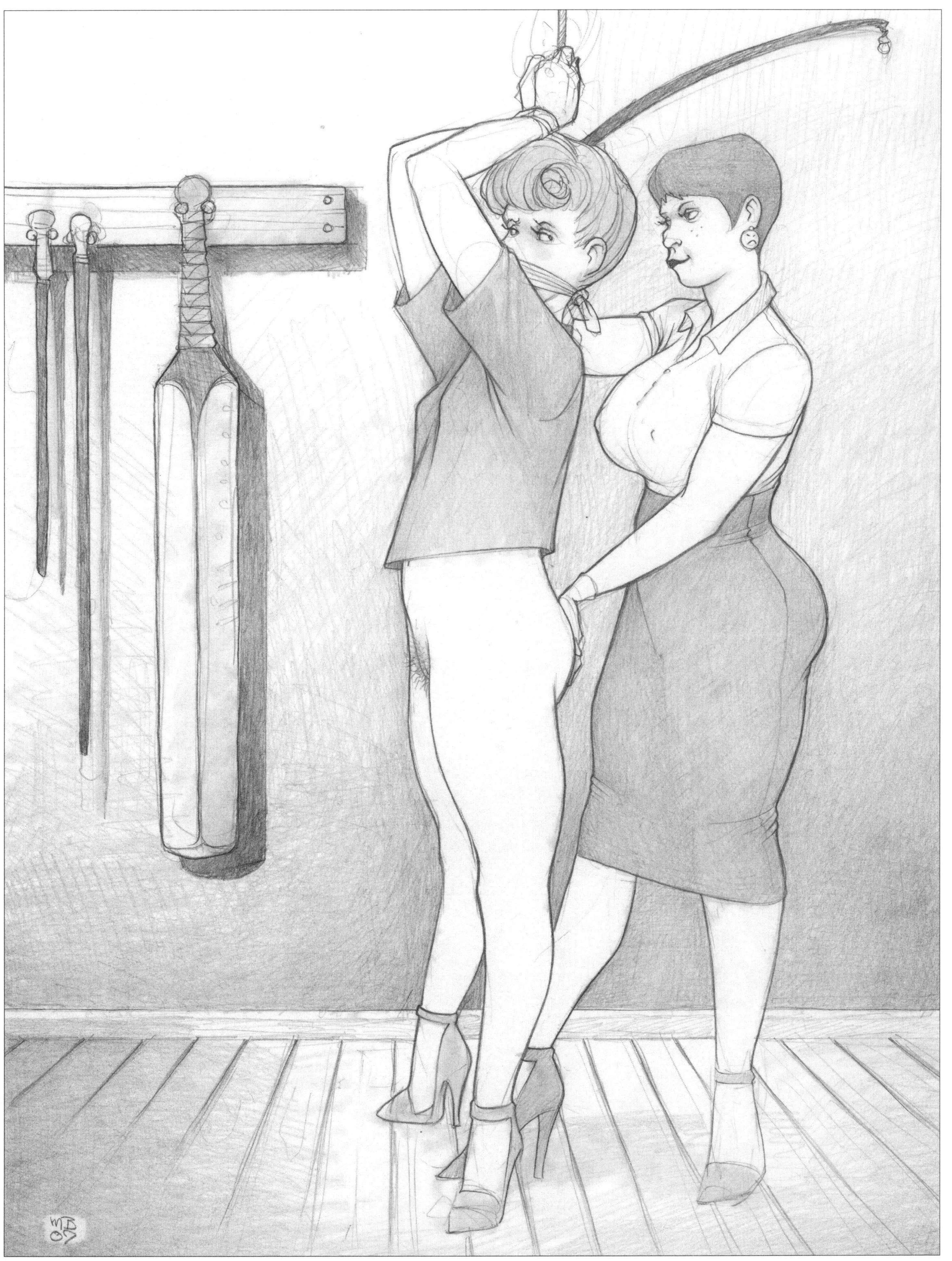

Mitch Byrd

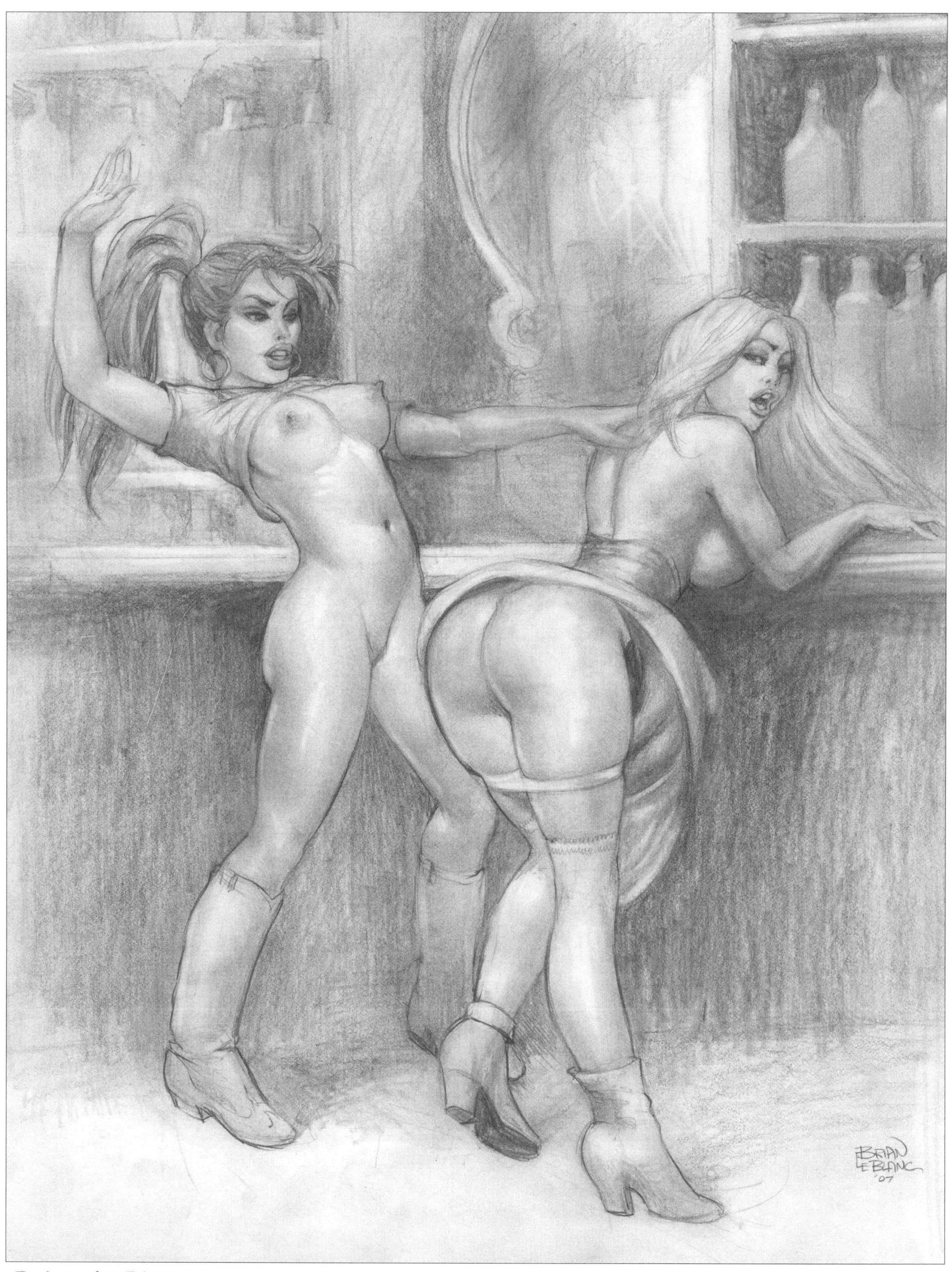

Brian LeBlanc

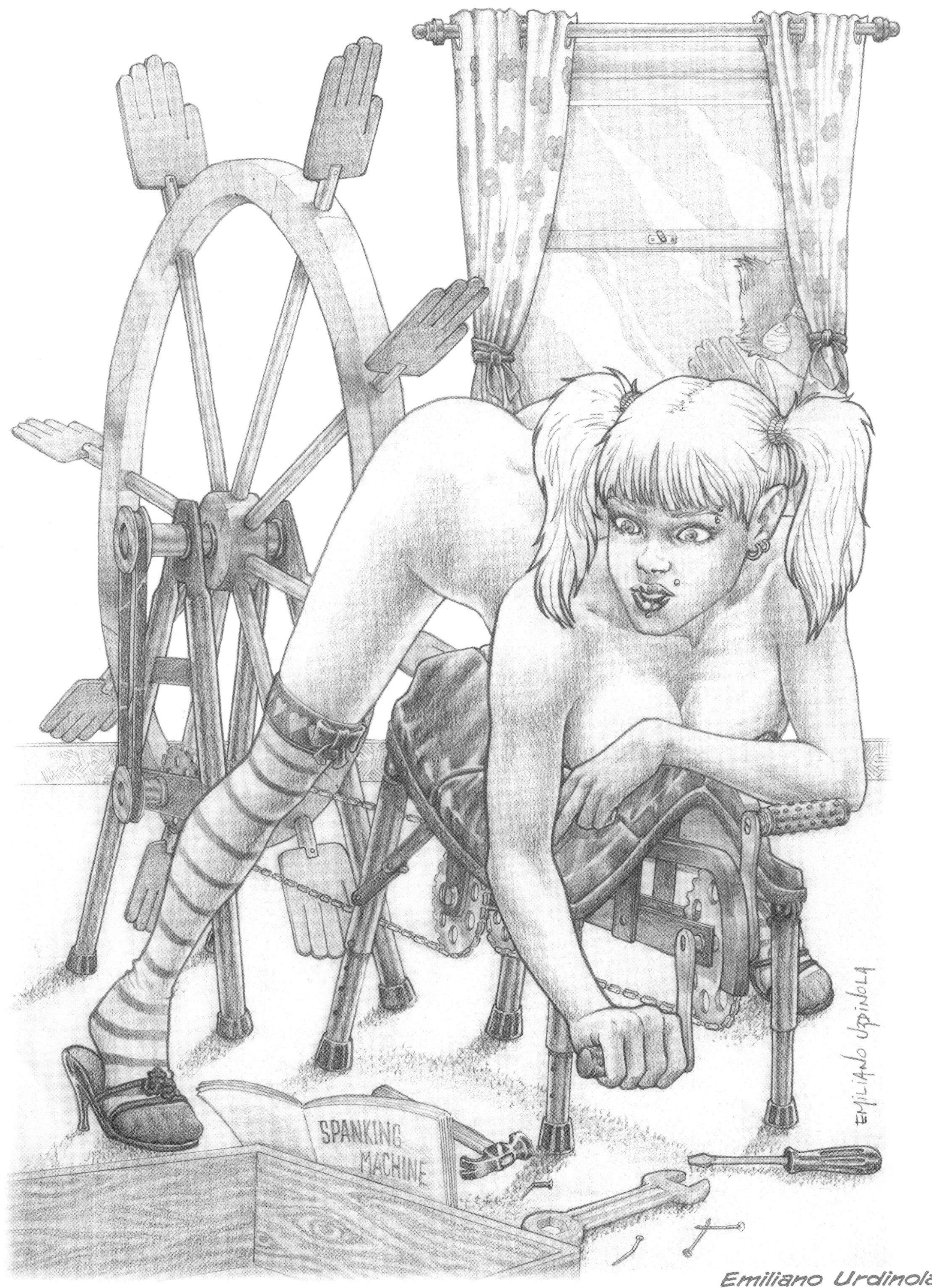

Emiliano Urdinola

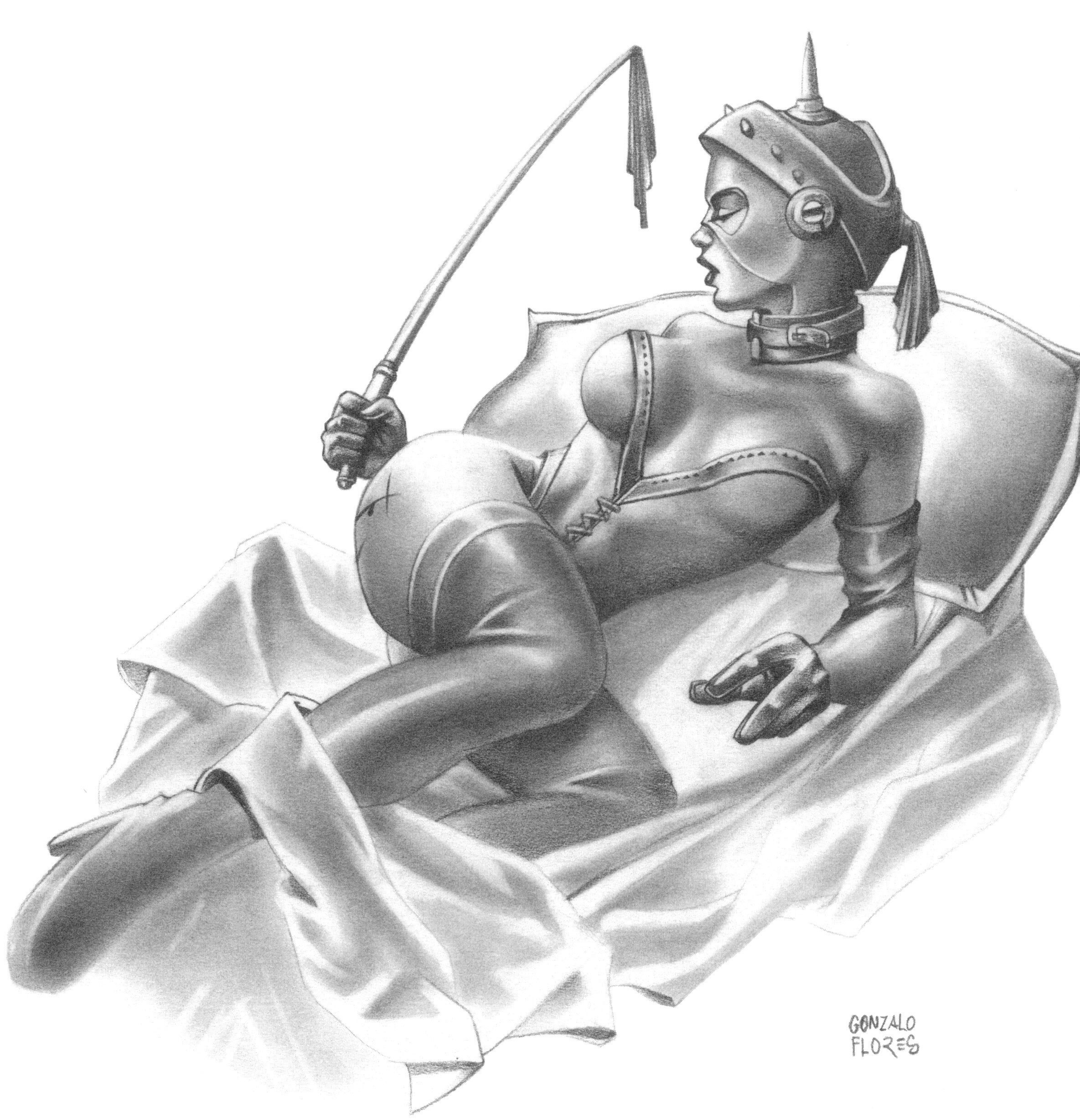

Gonzalo Flores

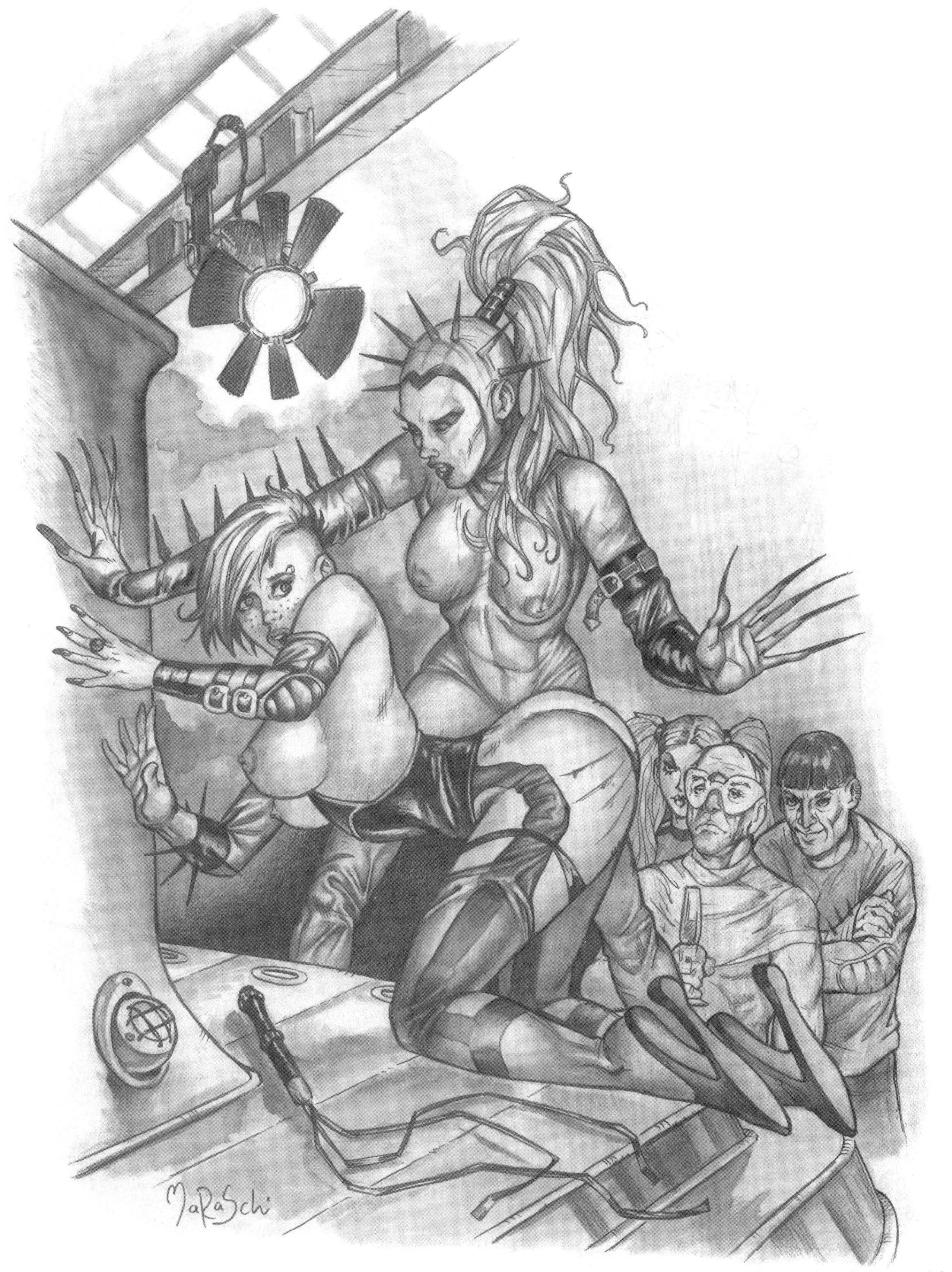

Anibal Maraschi

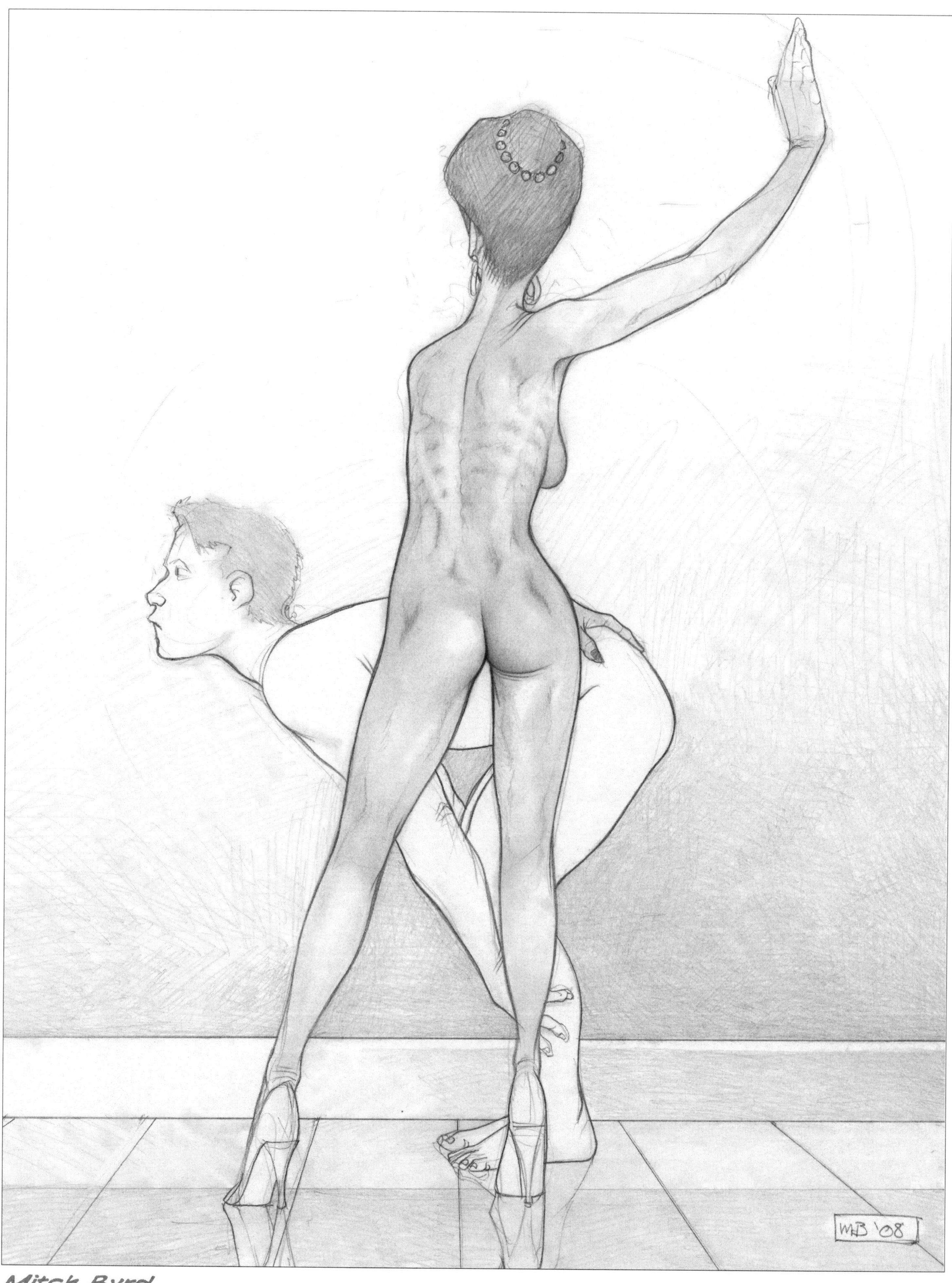

Mitch Byrd

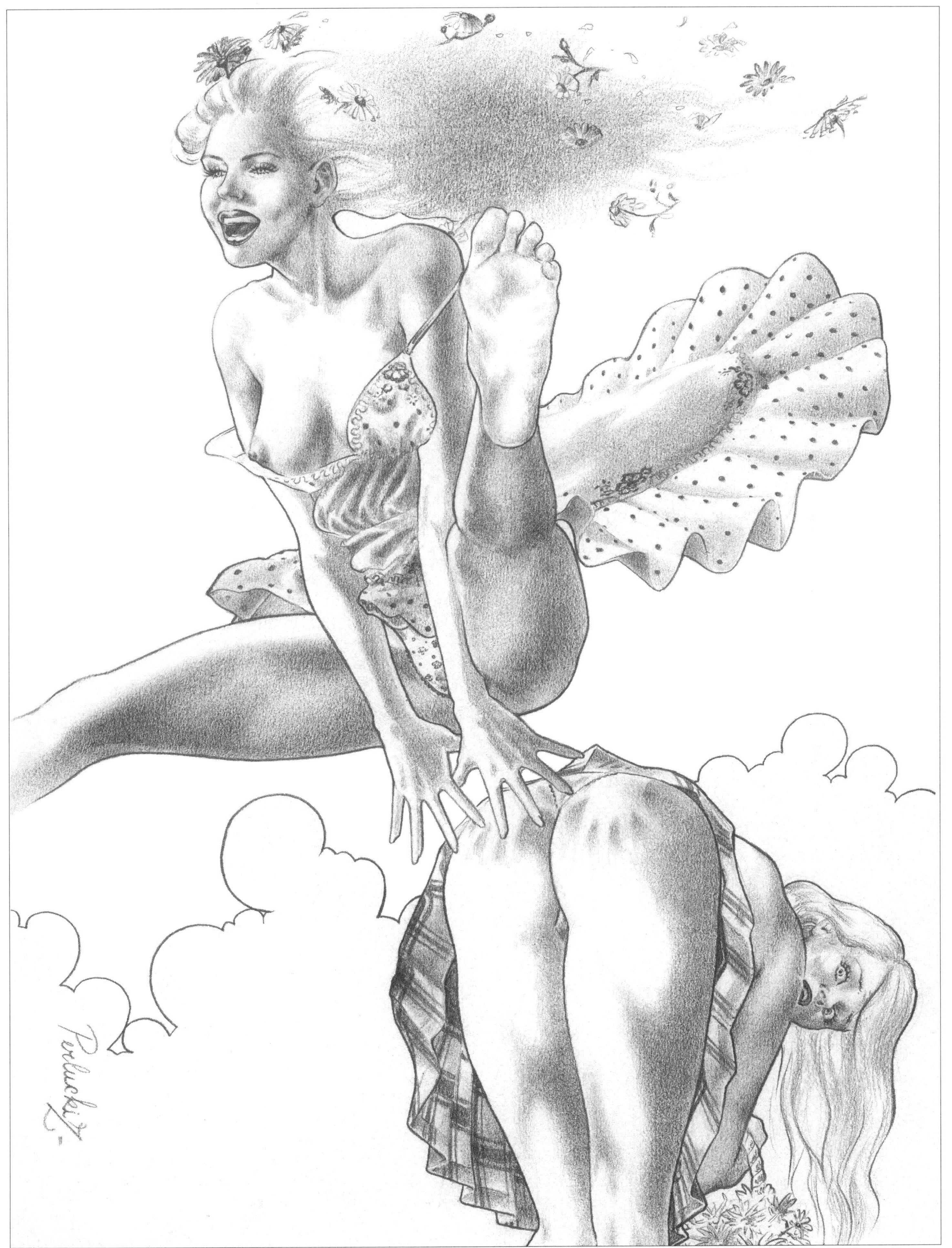

Perla Pilucki

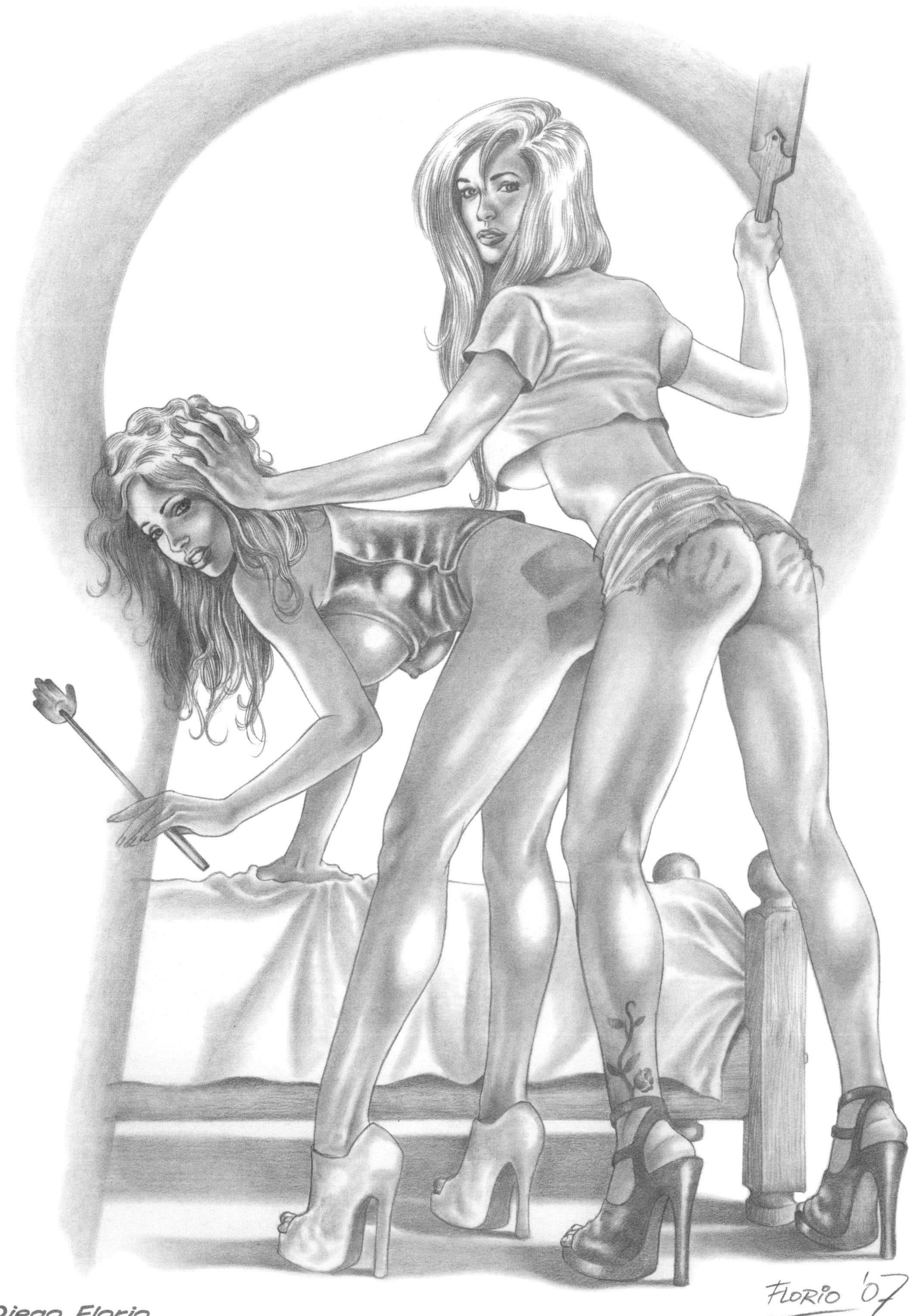

Diego Florio

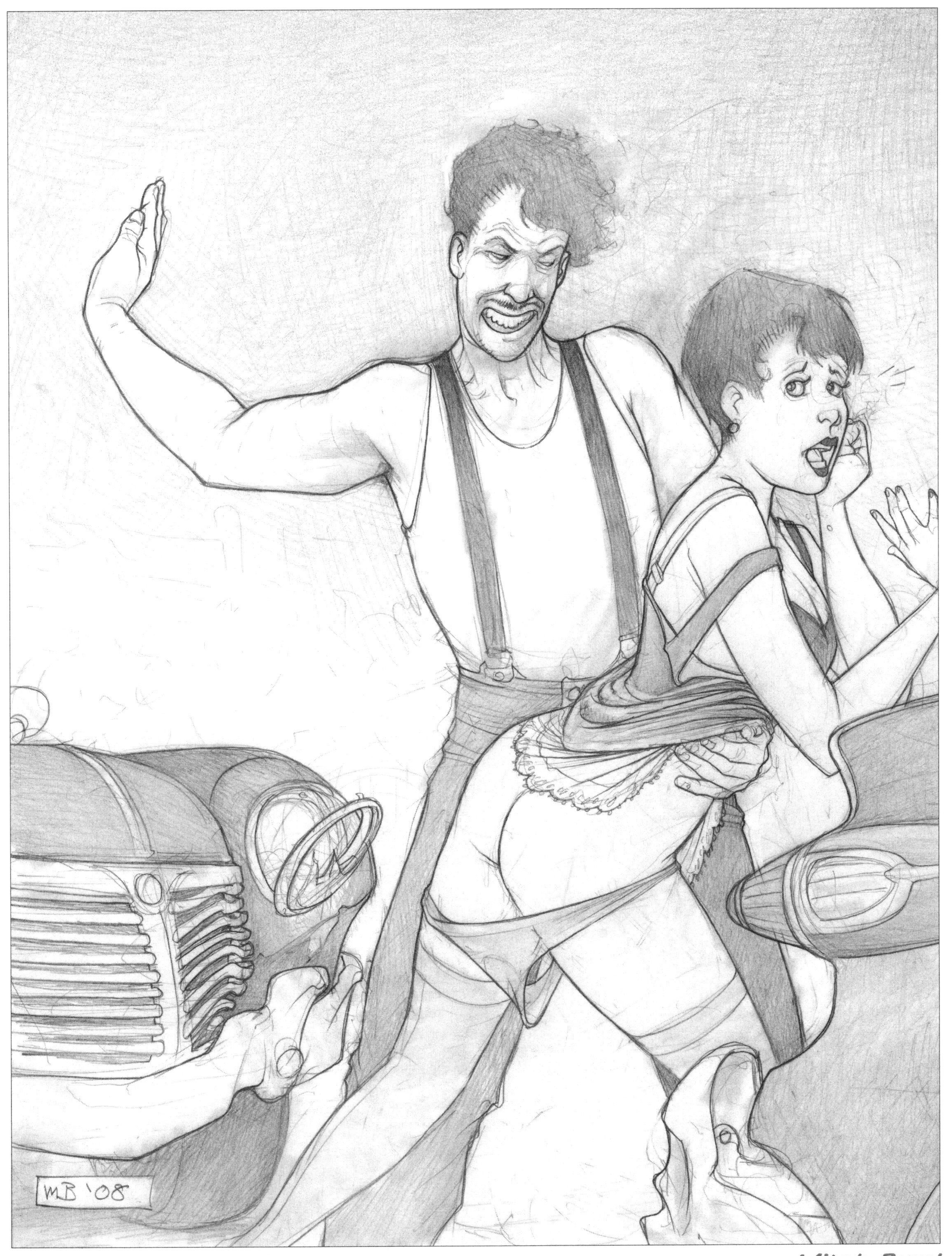

Mitch Byrd

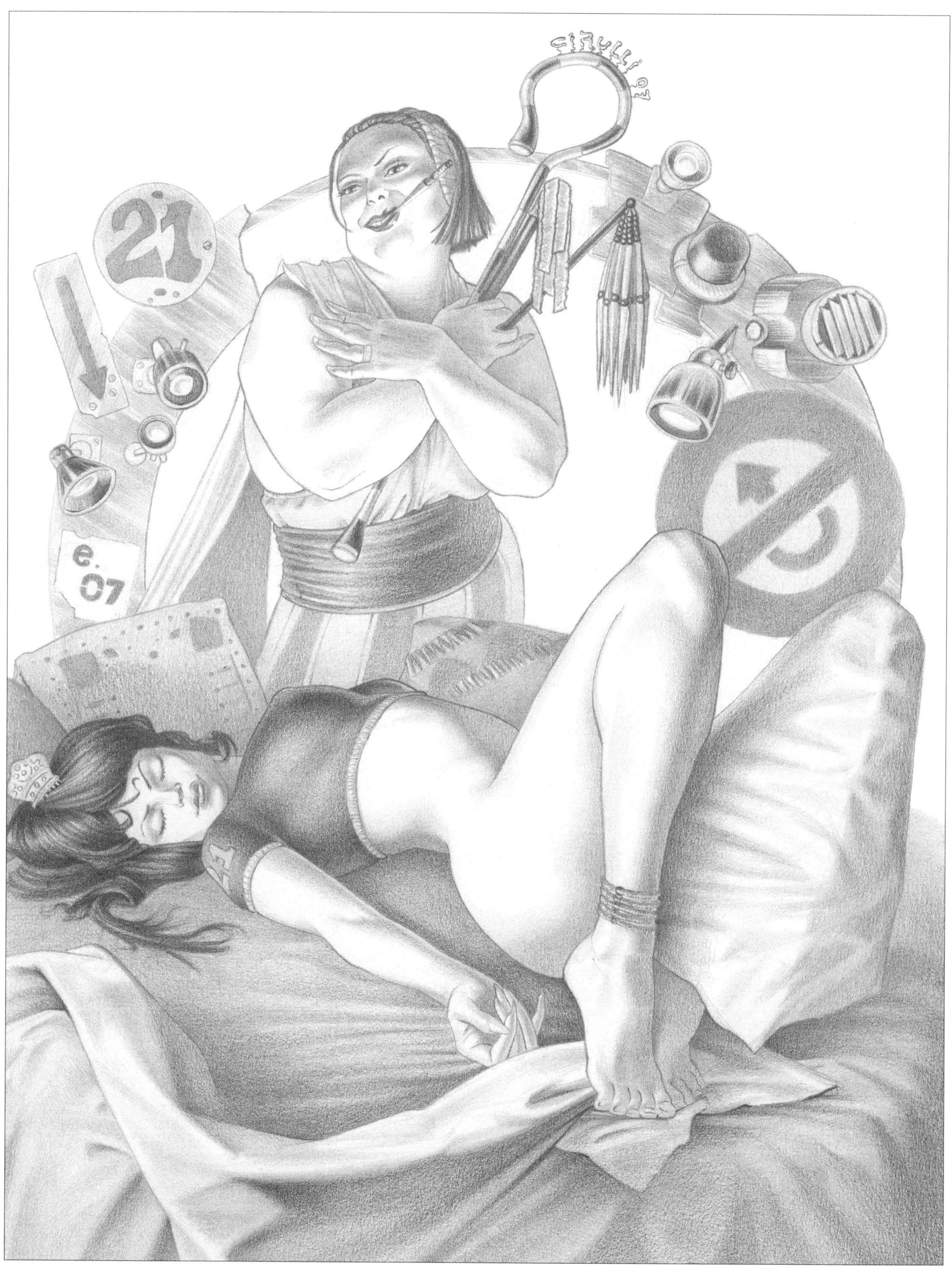

Diego Cirulli

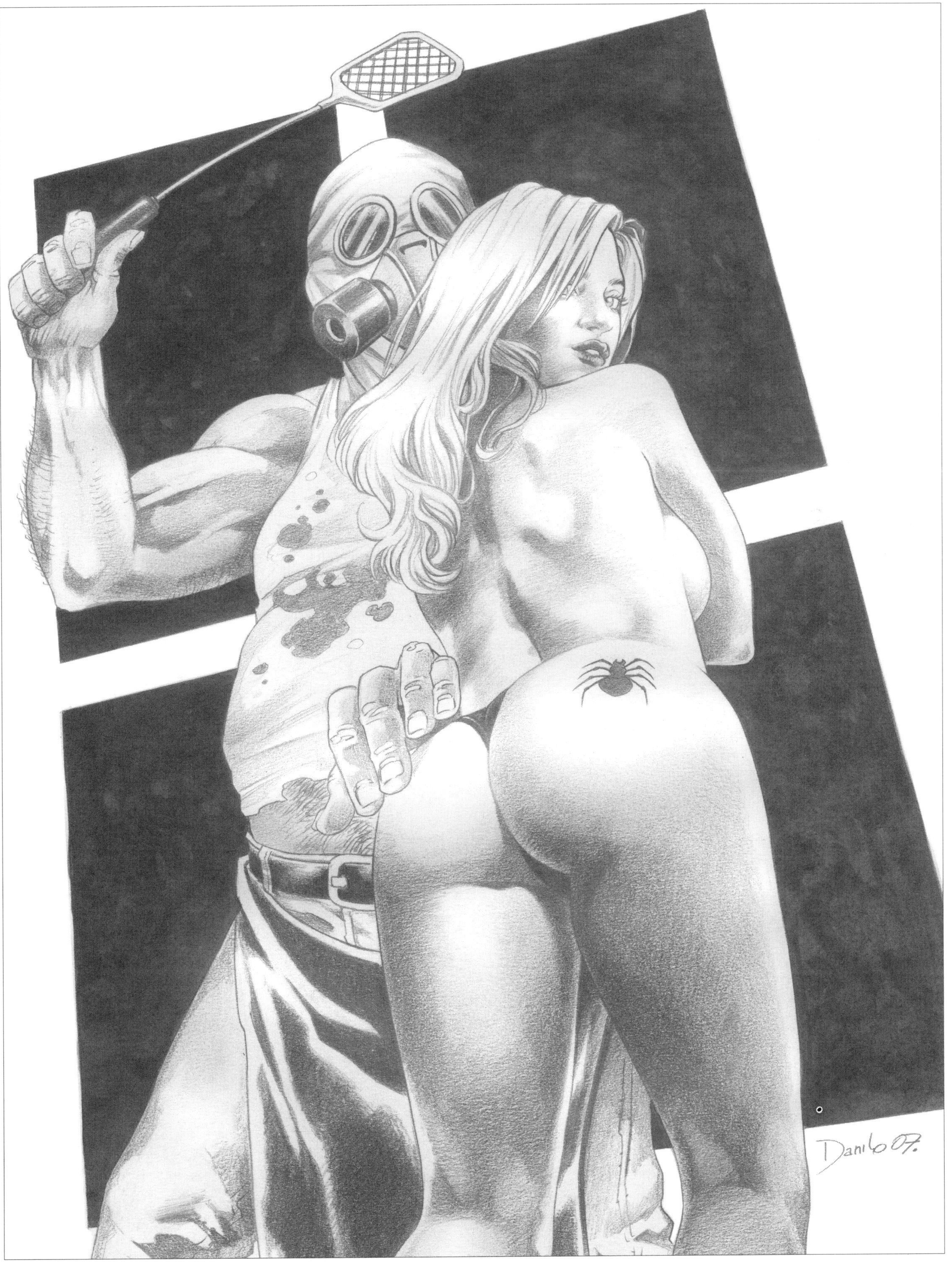

Danilo Guida

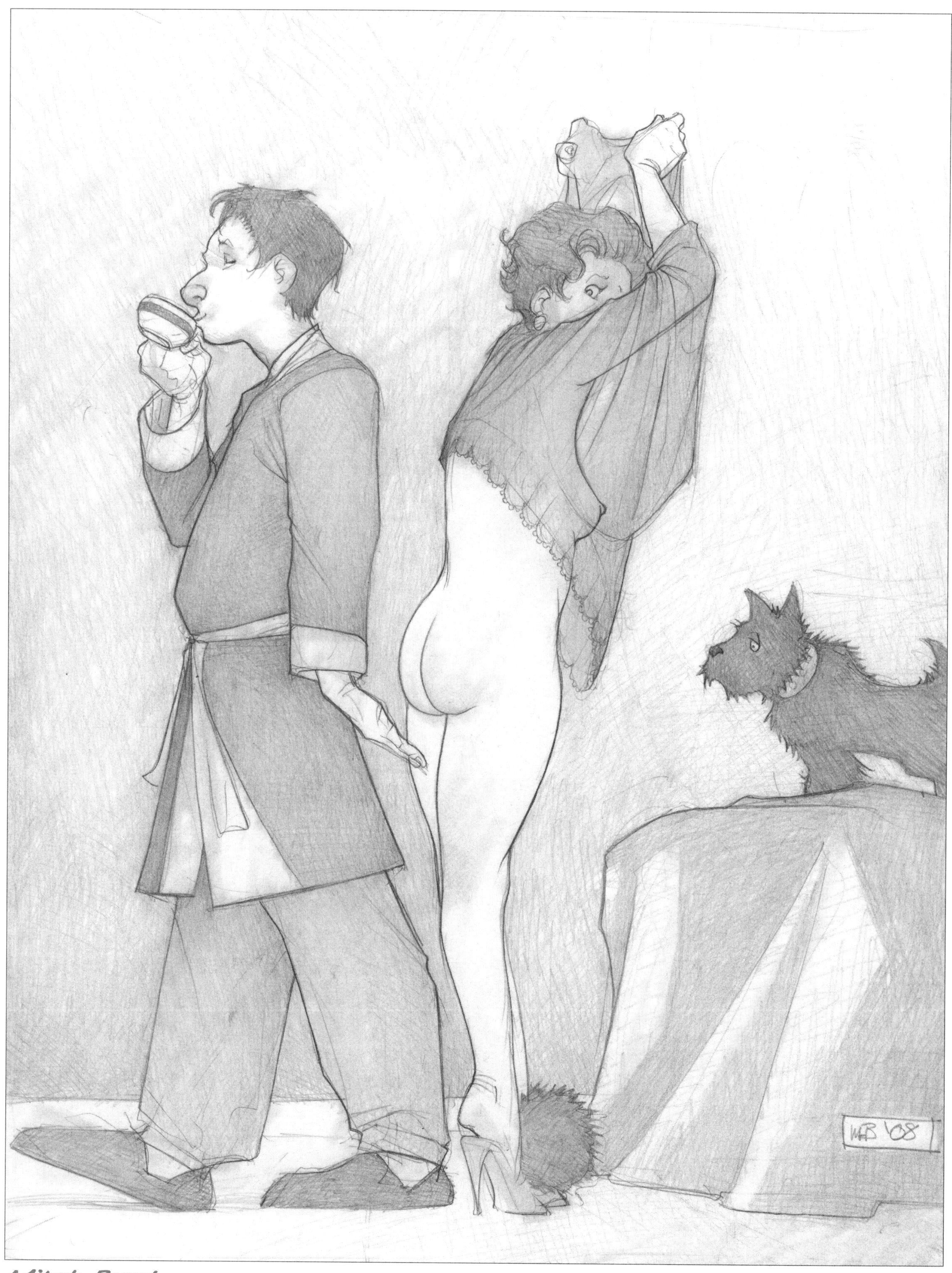

Mitch Byrd

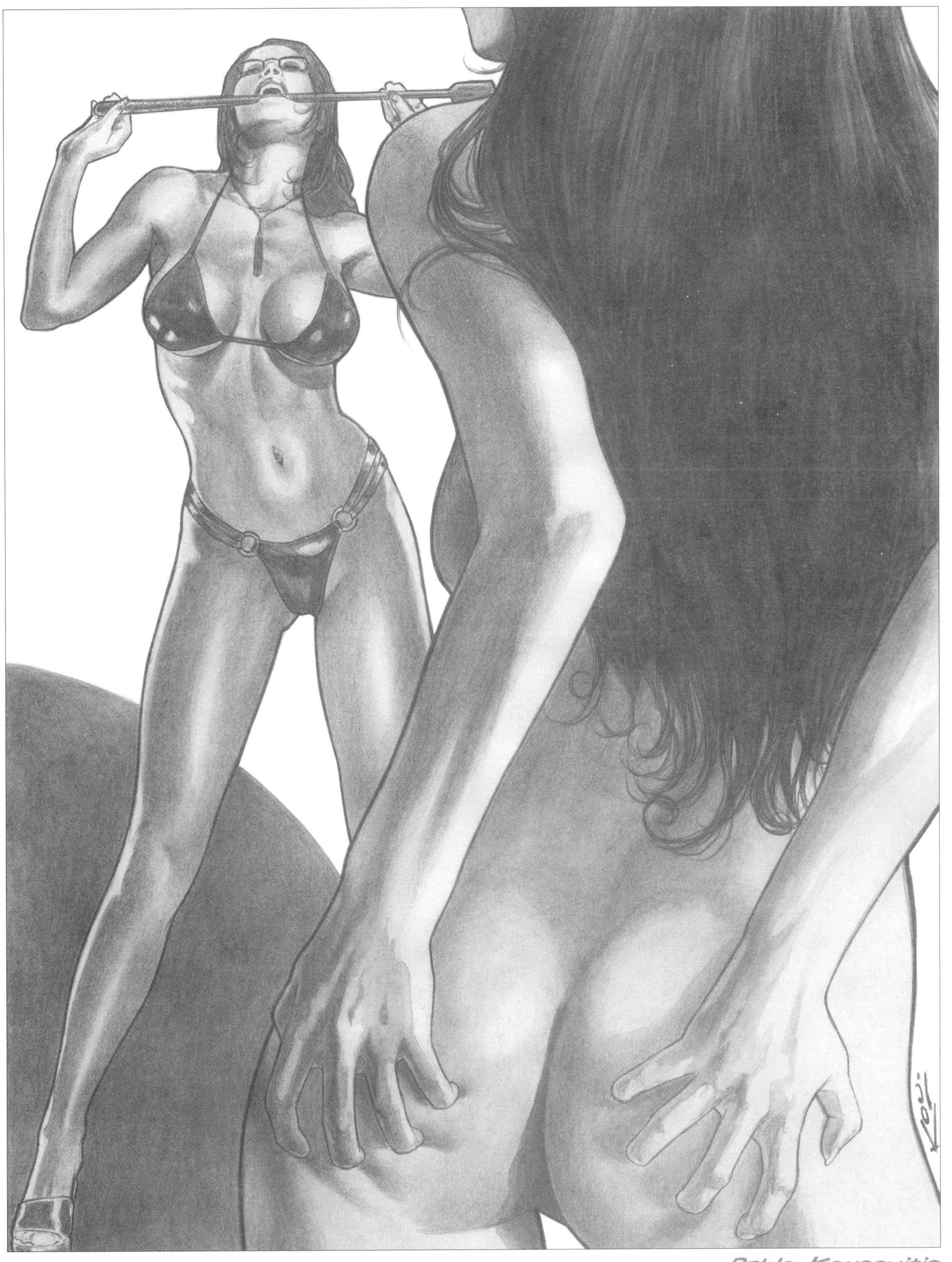

Pablo Kousovitis

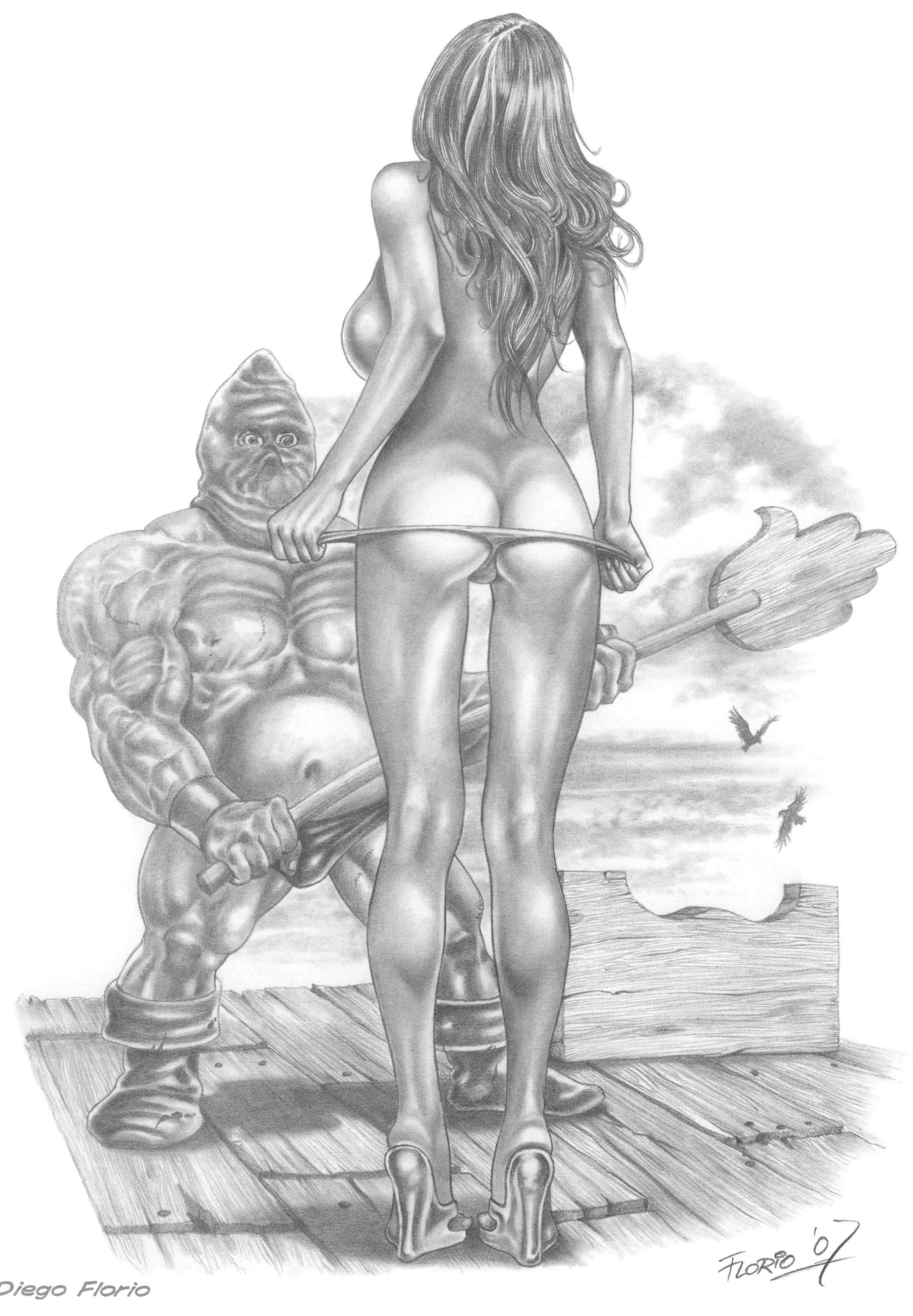

Diego Florio

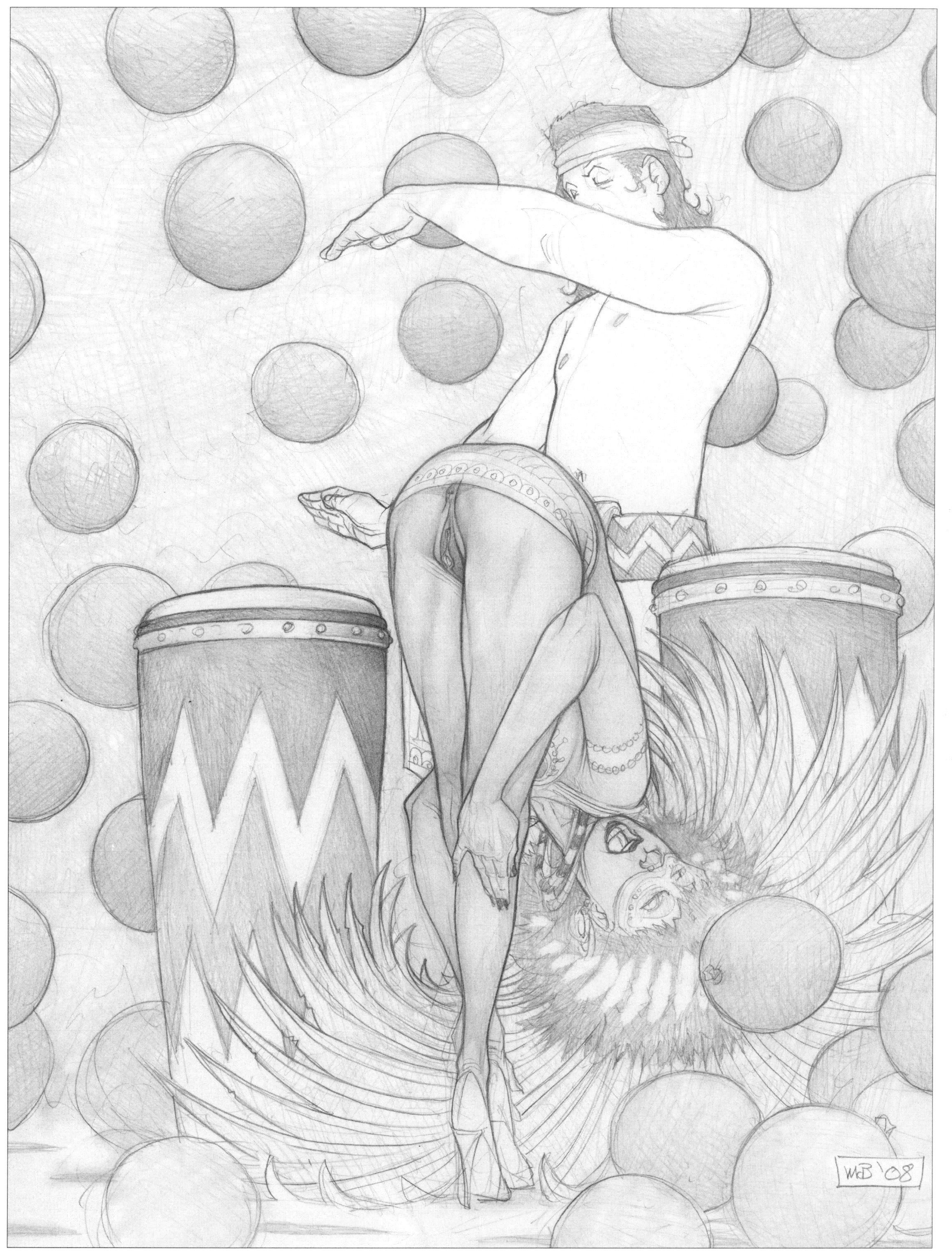

Mitch Byrd

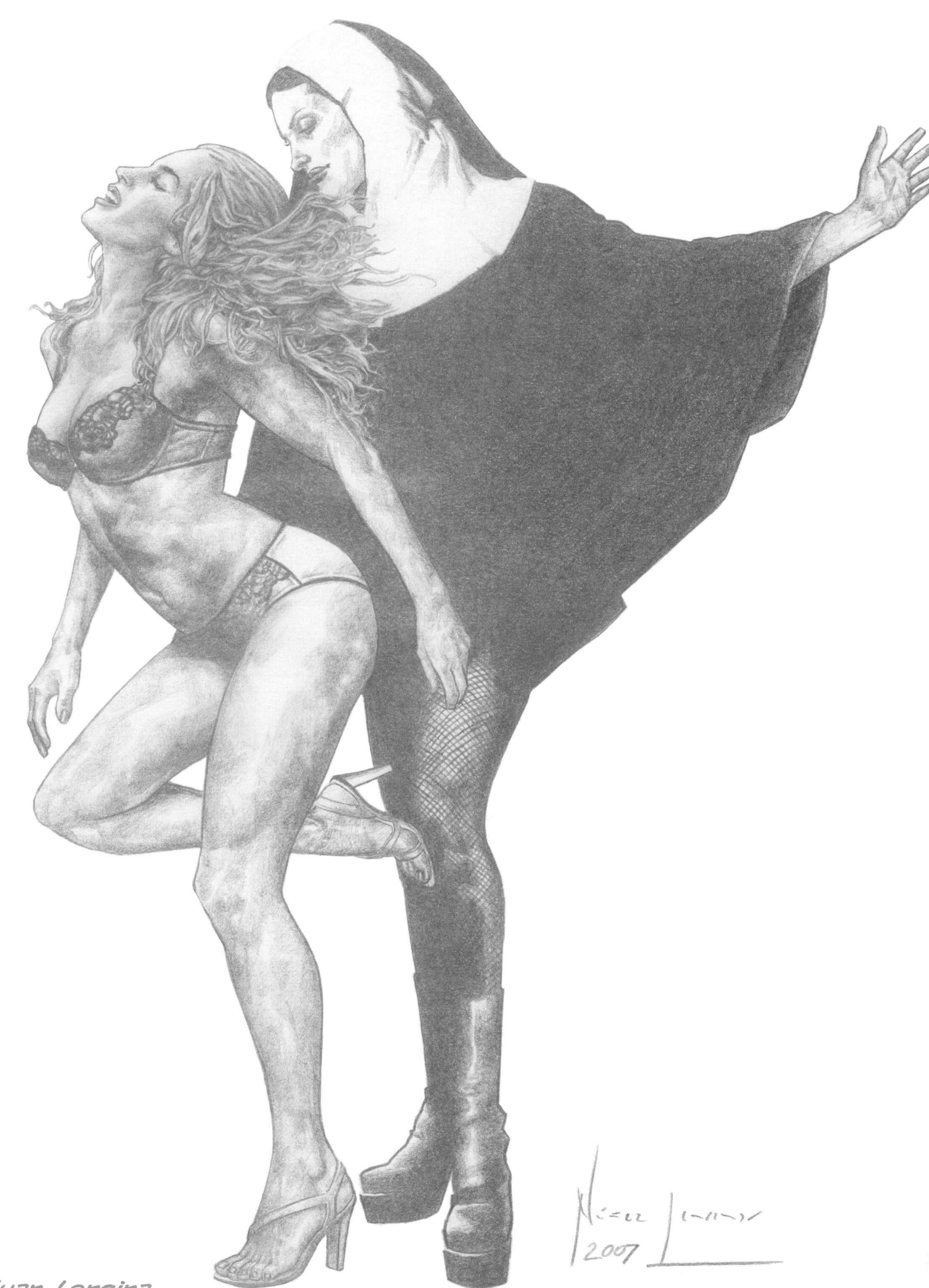

Juan Lencina

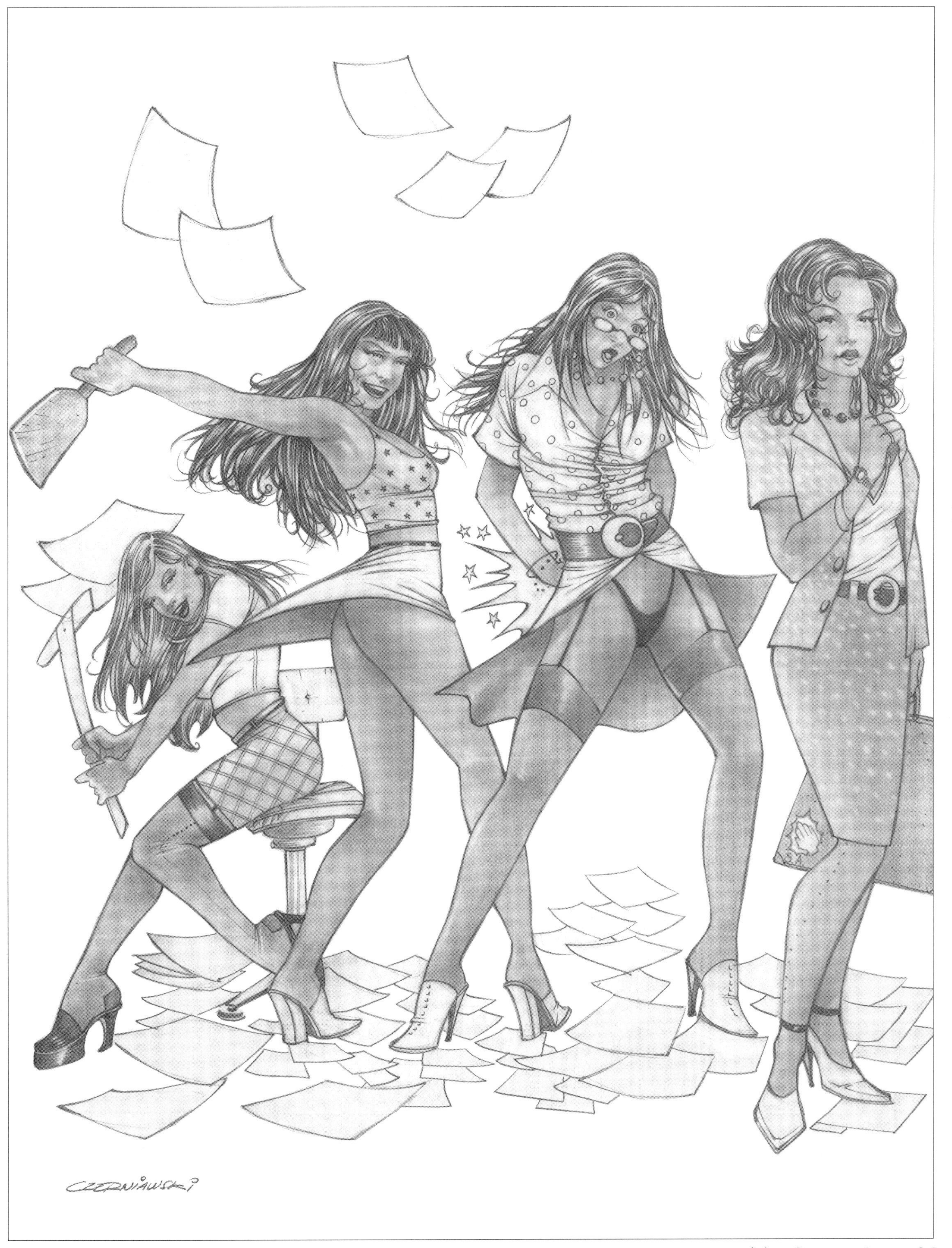

J.L. Czerniawski

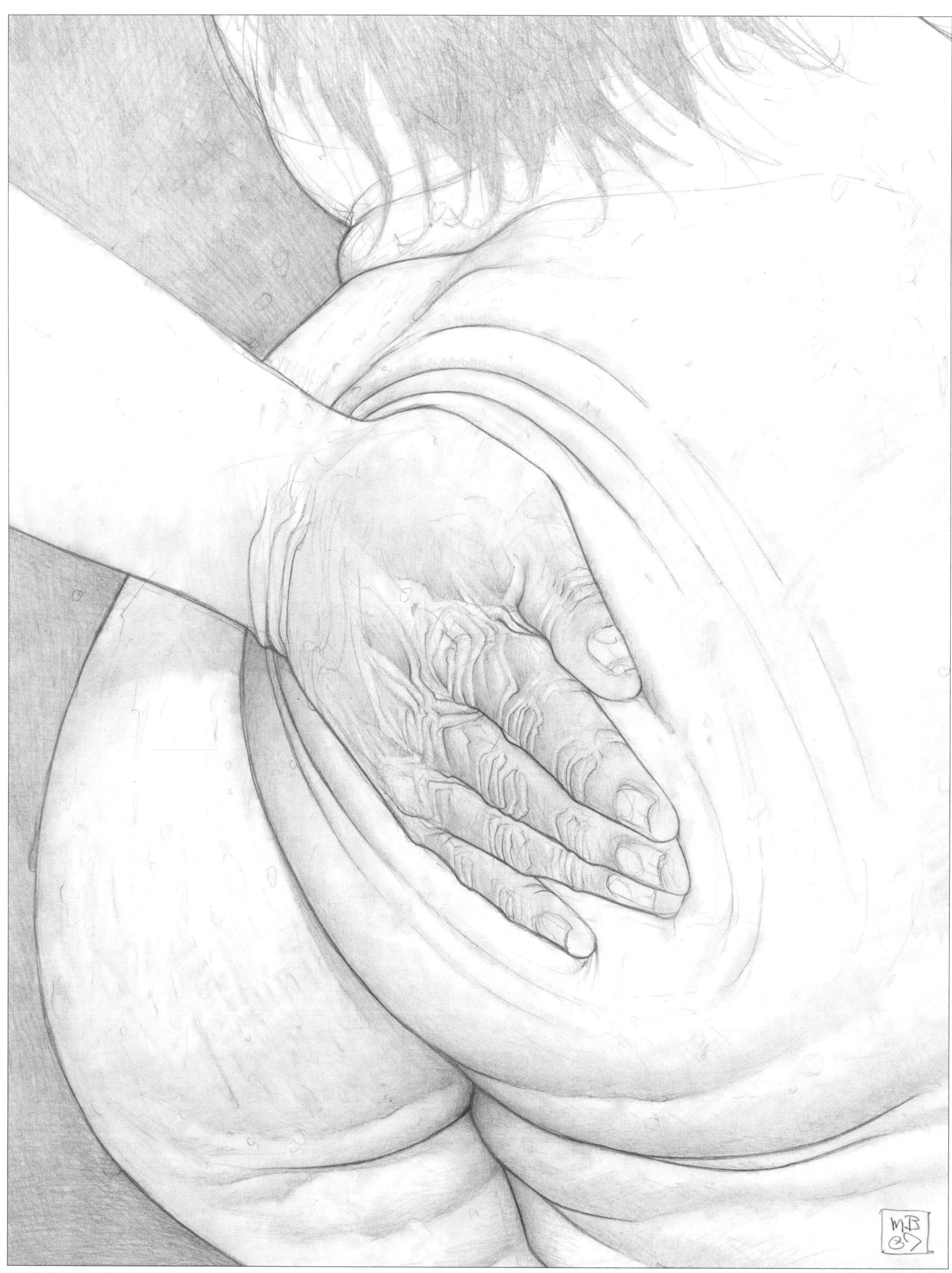

Mitch Byrd